How To Start

MAKING MONEY

With Your

DECORATIVE PAINTING

How To Start

MAKING MONEY

With Your

DECORATIVE PAINTING

DOROTHY EGAN

NORTH LIGHT BOOKS
CINCINNATI, OHIO

How to Start Making Money With Your Decorative Painting. Copyright
© 1998 by Dorothy Egan. Printed and bound in the United States of
America. All rights reserved. No part of this book may be reproduced in
any form or by any electronic or mechanical means including information
storage and retrieval systems without permission in writing from the
publisher, except by a reviewer, who may quote brief passages in a review.
Published by North Light Books, an imprint of F&W Publications, Inc.,
1507 Dana Avenue, Cincinnati, Ohio 45207. (800) 289-0963. First edition.

Other fine North Light Books are available from your local bookstore or
direct from the publisher.

02 01 00 99 98   5 4 3 2 1

Library of Congress Cataloging-in-Publication Data

Egan, Dorothy.
  How to start making money with your decorative painting / by Dorothy
Egan.—1st ed.
      p.   cm.
  Includes index.
  ISBN 0-89134-820-4 (pbk.)
  1. Painting. 2. Decorative and ornament. 3. Home-based businesses—
Management. I. Title.
TT385.E338   1998
745.7′23′068—dc21   98-11778
                                                        CIP

Edited by Kathy Kipp and Heather Farrow
Production edited by Amanda Magoto
Interior designed by Sandy Kent

The publisher gratefully acknowledges permission to reprint the forms on pages
14, 15, 51, 60-64.

✣ ABOUT THE AUTHOR ✣

Dorothy Egan has been involved with arts and crafts most of her life. Her decorative painting career began as a matter of economy, restoring old furniture. She has exhibited and sold her art at many conventions and craft shows. It was through selling at shows that she decided to publish her first book, *Take a Gander*. She has authored or co-authored over thirty books, including *Painting and Decorating Birdhouses* (North Light Books, 1997) and is a regular contributor to several magazines. Dorothy also has taught classes throughout the United States and Canada.

✤ ACKNOWLEDGMENTS ✤

I am deeply grateful to the people at F&W Publications for giving me the opportunity to write this book. They are a unique group because many of them are artists as well as editors. They understand the words they are editing and the world of decorative painting. A special thanks to Greg Albert, whose great outline gave me an easy, logical way to present the material in this book. Without his help I might still be writing the introduction. Thanks also to Kathy Kipp and Heather Farrow for their encouragement and patient editing of the manuscript.

My special thanks go to all of the artists who shared their experiences and allowed me to include them as examples of the various paths taken by decorative painters. I also want to thank the businesspeople who patiently answered my questions.

Finally, thank you to the Society of Decorative Painters for helping us find an avenue for sharing knowledge and information through local chapters and national conventions.

Introduction

Have you ever wondered if you could make money with your decorative painting skills? The answer is definitely yes, but not without knowledge, planning and maybe even a bit of luck.

Decorative painting usually begins as a hobby, something you do for pleasure. When you decide to make money with your painting it becomes a business. The most successful and satisfied painters integrate the two. To do this, you need to define your goals. Remember, success is not always measured by dollars. Many artists measure success by the skill levels they achieve. The money earned is a bonus that helps to meet the expenses incurred gaining those skills. If your goal is earning a living, you may be forced to sacrifice some of the personal satisfaction and relaxation found in painting for pleasure.

Before deciding on the business avenue you wish to pursue, think about your goals. Do you want a business that fits around everything else in your life but earns just enough money for your personal satisfaction? Are you career oriented and want to use this business as a major part or all of your income? This book will help you decide which option you wish to pursue and guide you in your quest as we consider the benefits and drawbacks of each business opportunity in the field of decorative painting.

We will begin by laying a good foundation and then work our way through what is needed in the superstructure of an entrepreneur. The first thing you may need to do is change your attitude about painting and business. Because painting usually begins as a hobby and evolves slowly into a business, it is easy to fall into an unprofessional work attitude, treating your painting as a hobby rather than a business. Those habits are difficult to break. It is essential to have the right attitude for success. If you want to earn money, you must think like a person in business, not a hobbyist. To have a successful business, you need to clearly define your goals and plan to reach them. Once you begin to look for markets, select the one best suited to your needs and personality.

Some people have innate marketing skills, and promoting their abilities comes as naturally as breathing. They see each and every business opportunity and have the ability to use those opportunities to their best advantage. They build a network of show promoters, gallery owners, publishers and anyone else who might afford them a chance to advance themselves and their abilities. Other people may not enjoy marketing but may thrive on personal contact with people, so they might function better working directly with the public at trade shows or teaching in a classroom situation. Still others may like to design and create but have no desire to teach or produce finished artwork to sell. Marketing their ideas in books and packets may be the route for them.

With the information in this book, you will be able to look honestly at your talents and have the knowledge to use your talents to your advantage. If you are a decorative painter with the desire to achieve, the opportunities are endless. The world is full of success stories. One of them could be yours.

Having the right attitude and confidence in yourself can be the difference between success and failure. Remember the story of Colonel Sanders. He was turned down hundreds of times before he found someone who thought he had a good idea. You probably won't need to be that persistent, but you may not be an instant success either. There are many opportunities out there. This book is the map to help you find that success.

CHAPTER ONE

Exploring Your Options

THERE ARE MANY WAYS to make money with your decorative painting. This chapter will discuss your options and help you understand their advantages and disadvantages. This will help you make an informed decision about which are right for you. However, be aware that the path you choose today may lead far afield from your planned destination, and "going with the flow" can open doors and reveal opportunities that you never dreamed possible. Many artists who had no plans beyond selling a few pieces at a local show were discovered by magazine editors and book publishers and have achieved national recognition and financial compensation far beyond their original goal. You will be able to achieve your goals if you are open to growth and new ideas.

Deciding how to apply your decorative painting skills is not always a clear path leading in one direction. It can be a gradually evolving process. Perhaps you have already been asked to sell pieces of your work or to teach a friend some of the basics of painting. Selling finished artwork and teaching are the two most popular methods of earning money with decorative painting. A relative or neighbor sees your work, likes it and asks to buy a piece or asks you to teach them how it was done, and before you know it, you're in business. Once that happens, the "domino effect" can begin, and your business will grow before you have a chance to organize your ideas and examine your options. So, before you settle into a routine of selling or teaching, let's briefly explore all the opportunities, the pros and cons of each, and give you some tips on selecting the right one for you so you can use your skills to the maximum advantage.

Define Your Goals

The first thing you need to do is define your goals. Ask yourself: Do you want to earn just enough to pay for supplies and classes, or do you want a business that pays your living expenses? Or somewhere between the two? Decide what you expect, then look at all your options. Do you want to sell your finished work, teach classes, create designs for books and/or packets or perhaps open a shop or studio? Let's do a little research and look at the many ways other painters apply their skills. This book will give you all the information, but, just like in school, you may have to do a little homework. You will need to check out the possible opportunities in your area.

I suggest you join a local chapter of the Society of Decorative Painters, talk to friends and go to craft shows, bazaars, malls, shops and anywhere else decorative painting is sold or taught. If publishing interests you, talk to someone who has produced books and packets. Try to attend a convention or seminar where decorative painting is featured. In other words, network! Other people who have "been there, done that" are literally your best resource. There are also many books with information about having a home-based business that, while not specific to decorative painting, can teach you about purchasing supplies, marketing, bookkeeping, taxes, etc. Check out your local bookstore and library.

Selling Finished Artwork

Most decorative painters start to paint for themselves, to decorate their homes and for relaxation. If you are a dedicated painter, there's a good chance you will produce more finished pieces than you can use. Selling your artwork can solve this problem. It can also earn you extra money to help pay for materials and classes. Another bonus is that by painting extra pieces, you practice your art and you can improve your skills much faster than if you paint only once or twice a week.

As your work improves, you might begin to give painted pieces as gifts. This introduces your work to a larger audience and opens the door to more requests. Then, someone asks if you sell your work. Soon a small market emerges. The feeling of being admired and appreciated, plus the newfound income, will inspire you to consider a larger market. And that's how it starts. "Mighty oaks from little acorns grow."

Looking for a Marketplace

After you sell your first pieces to friends or relatives, you will want to look for other outlets. These options will vary greatly, depending on where you live. Large cities naturally have more bazaars, shows, craft malls, etc. However, they can be oversaturated, which can make it more difficult to gain a large, loyal customer base. Smaller towns sometimes support artisans very well and can offer more opportunities than larger cities. In upcoming chapters, we will look at all the available outlets in detail and explore the pros and cons of each.

When you look for outlets for your art, the list is limited only by your imagination. You can have a small show in your home, sell your work at the office, display your work in a craft mall or go to weekend craft shows and flea markets. Be open to every opportunity that comes your way.

Don't be discouraged if your first attempt at selling your work is not successful. It takes experience to fully understand the people who want to buy your work. Certain styles of painting sell better in different parts of the country. Intricate, time-consuming work that requires a high selling price usually sells better when it is shown with other work of similar quality. Price is always a factor and needs to be considered when choosing a way to market your work. When you factor in the cost of materials and the time spent producing the finished work, you may discover that what you are doing is too "pricey" for the common marketplace. Look at your work critically and honestly before you look for a place to sell it. Be flexible, and add a few more affordable pieces that will have wider appeal.

Finding a Customer Base

It also takes time to build a clientele. One painter I know barely paid for her postage expense with her first home show. After five years, people were lined up for almost a city block when the show opened, and she sold out in a few hours. She did one-of-a-kind art that would become cherished family heirlooms, and people were willing to pay the price because she had the patience to build a clientele that understood and appreciated her work.

Having great painting skills is not the most important factor in success. I know several painters who sell out at show after show, not because of the *quality* of their painting but because they know and understand trends. They have a knack for creating a current and timely look. They watch style, color and what's fresh on the market. They create a look that people want. Some painters can do it with only basic skills, because their work is clever but simple. They don't spend a great deal of time on each piece, so it can be moderately priced.

Teaching

Another popular way to earn money is by teaching classes and sharing your knowledge with other painters. Years ago, when small shops flourished, teaching opportunities were more plentiful. Many painters who wanted to teach opened their own shops and had successful businesses generated by teaching classes and selling supplies. Now, in most parts of the country, your only choices are to teach in your home or in a large chain store.

To teach classes at home, you will need to provide certain basic elements. The first is adequate space, and the second is good lighting. If these are available, you need to consider other possible problems, such as zoning laws, parking, accessibility and availability of supplies, just to name a few. But teaching in your own home is a good place to begin and to develop teaching skills and lesson plans before moving into a more public marketplace.

More and more large craft stores are adding classroom space. They are learning that classes are the lifeblood of the business, because they create a steady demand for their products. If teaching interests you, don't hesitate to call on store managers to present your ideas and samples of your work. Remember, you have a great deal to offer them. Good classes promote sales in their store. If management is not ready for classes, you may need to be willing to donate your time or to do demonstrations in the store to prove your skills. This can be a wise investment of your time because it not only will show the management that there is interest in classes, but it also will introduce your work to the store's customer base.

Classes can be grouped several ways. Some stores offer ongoing classes, usually taught in sets of six to eight weeks. Others only want to offer workshops where a project is taught in each class. Some shops have a combination of both. Ongoing classes produce a steady, more predictable income, but workshops are sometimes easier to fill and more lucrative due to the sale of supplies. Most teachers charge more for a workshop than for ongoing classes. Workshops also can be a source of finding new students for ongoing classes.

There are other opportunities to teach for experienced teachers, such as conventions and seminars, and we will look at them in a later chapter.

Publishing

Publishing is an option if you have designing skills. The work must be original, and you must be able to draw patterns and to write clear instructions. But it is certainly a goal worth striving for. As you teach or paint to sell, you should add personal touches to your work to set it apart from other artists' work. After you develop your own personal style, you can begin to consider publishing your work in books or packets. If you've ever bought a book or packet with poor patterns or difficult-to-follow instructions, you know how frustrating that can be. So, if publishing is one of your goals, develop your writing talents as you improve your painting skills.

Breaking Into Print

Publishing can be a very risky business. I know several artists who suffered great financial losses because they went into it without enough preparation and forethought. It is definitely the outlet of choice for many artists, but it needs to be approached with baby steps, not giant strides.

Where to Begin

Producing packets is a good way to test the market and is much less of a financial risk than publishing a book. Another option is to submit your work to magazines. They pay you for each design, and it is an excellent way to get national exposure for your work. It also gives you an unbiased evaluation of your work. Finally, there are publishers who handle groups of artists. They publish and distribute the books and pay the artist a royalty. Last on my list is self-publishing. It's a risky business and not for the fainthearted.

Home Decorating

Everyone knows what it is to be commissioned to paint a picture. In past years that usually meant being hired to paint a specific painting. Now it more commonly means being hired to work in the area of home decorating. As faux finishes and trompe l'oeil gain popularity, the opportunities for decorative painters increase as well. Many painters find full-time outlets for their skills by working with decorators and builders, doing faux finishes, stenciling and hand-painted details in clients' homes.

Painted furniture is another popular item that presents the decorative painter with new opportunities. Think about all of the painted pieces you see in decorating magazines and catalogs, and you will begin to understand the opportunities. From painting on new furniture to refinishing vintage pieces, there is a large market for skilled, imaginative artists.

As you can see, there are many ways to make money with your decorative painting. Selecting the right one is a personal decision, and no one can make it for you. Use this book to *help* you make that decision. So, now that you know your options, you are ready to proceed to the next chapters for a closer look at the opportunities that await you.

CHAPTER TWO

Selling at Shows

SELLING FINISHED WORK is the most popular way to earn money with your painting skills. We'll begin by covering the way most people get started. Beyond selling to friends and relatives, there is selling at shows. Selling at shows actually covers a variety of ways to introduce your painted work into the marketplace. Let's define a show as an affair where you display your work for a certain period of time, selling it directly to the public at a retail price. There are many kinds of shows—private and public, very small to very large—and each type has assets and liabilities that need consideration.

There are advantages to selling at shows. They can enlarge your customer base and build a clientele that will support you in future years. But there are disadvantages too. The physical effort that goes into doing shows is great and can be too much work for some people. Shows are also seasonal (typically they are popular during the spring and fall) so your income is not constant. Of course, if you are not dependent on a steady income, you can use the in-between time to paint and prepare for the next selling season. In spite of these few drawbacks, shows are still the most well-established and popular way for artists to sell their work.

Each kind of show has appealing qualities and certain requirements that need consideration. Let's take a look at the various kinds of shows.

Church and School Bazaars

One of the first places many artists try to sell their work is a church or school bazaar. Booth fees are usually low, and they are almost always one-day events. The expense and stress levels are also fairly low. It's an easy way to test the market and get your feet wet.

If possible, attend the show at least once before deciding to take part in it. Due to timing, location, advertising and sponsorship, this type of

A number of publications list craft shows for the upcoming year. They divide the information by area, so you receive a comprehensive list of arts and crafts shows in a certain zone. They contain information such as show dates, locations, booth fees, entry deadlines, estimated attendance and contact information. They also include advertisements from sources for craft show supplies, such as tents, canopies, plastic bags, etc. Contact:

The ABC Directory of Arts and Crafts Events
P.O. Box 5388, Maryville, TN 37802-5388, (800) 678-3566

Craft Fare Magazine
P.O. Box 1496, Oak Lawn, IL 60453, (708) 430-3033

event can vary *greatly* from show to show. Some shows are very small and not well attended. Others open to large crowds eagerly waiting to purchase quality items. If the show has a lot of vendors who sell inexpensive, very crafty projects, your work may not fit in and may seem overpriced by comparison. However, the quality of your work may stand out from the others and sell very well. The only way to find out is to give it a try.

Sometimes shows of this nature furnish only the bare essentials for a booth, frequently just a table. You will need something to cover the table and, if you have hanging artwork, a backdrop or display board. As with any sale, you should be prepared with basic items such as price tags, business cards, bags, tissue or suitable wrapping supplies, pens, ticket books and any tools needed to set up your booth. A complete supply list is covered on page 28.

Private Shows

Another vehicle for sales is having a show in your own home or the home of a friend. If you decide to try this method, it's probably wise to make it "by invitation only," limiting it to acquaintances and their friends. It would be unwise to open a private home to complete strangers by general advertising, but be sure to add "Bring a friend" to the invitation to increase the number who will attend.

You can also have a group of artist friends get together to have a private home show. Each participant supplies a list of friends to be invited. This works well because it creates a broader customer base, and there is a wider variety of merchandise to interest the customers.

Tips for Home Show Success

Invitations

The rules of home shows are simple but absolutely essential to success. It begins with the invitation—the customer's first impression of your show. Word-of-mouth can be moderately successful, but a printed or handwritten invitation lends importance to the event and is a better reminder. Whether your invitation is colorful or elegant, it should enhance the mood of the sale. Strive to make it memorable. If you have a logo or theme, use it throughout the sale, from the invitations to the design on the bags in which you put the merchandise that is sold. You want to create an image in the mind of your customers.

Display

Display your items well. A private home is a wonderful showcase for your work because it allows people to see it in the environment where it will be used. Be sure you tag your artwork clearly so they will know it is for sale and not just part of the decor. If you use shelves or display tables, arrange your finished work so it looks inviting, not like you are having a tag sale. Price tags should be easily visible. It's always wise to use hangtags and even wiser to use hangtags that are interesting and distinctive.

Record Keeping

Keep good records of both expenses and sales, especially if it is a group sale. After the show, you don't want to deal with disputes over what sold and who gets the money. The expenses incurred should be split among the participants in the sale and should be deducted or paid before any of the money is divided.

It is wise to record the names and addresses of all people who pay by check. These names will be the foundation of your future invitation list. If a guest, after being invited twice, fails to come or comes but never spends money, eliminate that name from your list. One very successful home show group uses this principle. They add new names by recording new guests who pay by check and always add "Bring a friend" to every invitation. After a few years, they have such an eager following, they have to shorten

Carol Mays
Carol's booth at the Heart of Ohio Tole Convention shows how easy it is to set up a pleasing and exciting display. Lighting helps draw attention to her pattern packets. Carol also does demonstrations in her booth, which gets people to stop and watch what she's doing.

the hours of their show because they sell out early at each show.

One of the advantages of having a private home sale is that your expenses are relatively low. Of course, if you "do it with style" the expenses are often about the same as for a church or school bazaar. However, at home you can display your art without competition from other exhibitors and build a clientele that is devoted to your work. Sometimes the first show may not be as successful as expected, but you can learn with each effort. If you do it right, you will soon develop a customer base that appreciates the quality of work offered and anxiously awaits each show.

Regional Craft Shows

In most areas of the country, there are large craft fairs or shows that last from two to five days. They usually draw huge crowds from surrounding states. The advantage of these shows is that these crowds come prepared to spend money. One of the disadvantages is that there is a lot of competition. Often several shows are going on at the same time in the same general area, so there may be a number of people with work similar to yours. Another disadvantage is that often these shows are in locations where exhibitor expenses run high. You need to consider booth fees, commissions, lodging, meals and travel expenses. These costs need to be factored into your selling price.

Many of the large shows are juried shows where a panel of judges reviews slides or photographs of your work before you are accepted as an exhibitor. A popular show may have a waiting list, or you may not be accepted on your first try. Don't give up. If it is very selective, it will be worth the wait.

Large weekend shows rarely furnish anything but space. Occasionally, a roof overhead will be provided. You may need to furnish your own tables, backdrop, lighting, etc. If it is an outdoor show, you will definitely want an umbrella, tent or canopy. Sun and rain can cause serious damage to your merchandise. Large indoor trade shows and conventions usually have a service company available that rents supplies and helps set up and take down—for a fee.

Holiday Houses

Many cities have civic groups whose yearly fund-raiser is a show and sale held for a time in an unoccupied house during the holiday season. These holiday houses are usually open for four to six weeks. The sponsoring group takes a percentage of your sales and, in return, handles setup, sales and restocking, so your only involvement is producing pieces to sell and replacing items in hot demand. Although the take-out percentage may be fairly high, remember the sponsors are doing all the advertising, stocking, etc. This frees your time and money for other things. Exhibitors are usually chosen for these shows by a committee trying to balance the selection of merchandise, which means they will limit the number of artists or craftspeople doing similar work.

Choosing the Right Show

Where to Look for Shows

If you love decorative painting, there is a good chance you have already attended shows where other artists exhibit and sell. If so, you may already have some shows in mind or at least know where to begin. If you aren't familiar with what is available, it's time to do some homework.

To find shows, begin by asking other painters or inquire at your favorite supply shop or where you take classes. Read the newspaper, both the classified section and the local events listings. Check with the chamber of commerce in your hometown and in the surrounding area.

**EXHIBITOR SPACE PRE-REGISTRATION
26TH ANNUAL CONVENTION - PHOENIX, AZ
JUNE 2 - 7, 1998**

**Society of Decorative Painters
393 N McLean Blvd
Wichita, KS 67203
Phone: 316.269.9300 Fax: 316.269.9191**

Membership Number: _____

Business Name: _____

Address: _____

City: _____ State: _____ Zip: _____

Phone: _____ Fax: _____

E-Mail Address: _____

Number of Booths reserved for Phoenix (max 3) _____

Deposit Paid ($200.00 per Booth): _____

Check: _____ Visa: _____ Mastercard: _____

Credit Card Number: _____ Expires: _____

Signature: _____

I Would Like To Reserve _____ Corner Booth(s). Each corner booth will be an additional $50.00 payable with your contract. No additional deposit for a corner booth is required now. The amount of corner booths is determined by the layout at the Convention Center. Corner booths will be assigned in the following manner: (1) If you have reserved 1 or 2 on this form, (2) If your balance due payment is received by the Contract deadline. We will make every effort to assign you a corner booth if you have pre-reserved one but we do not guarantee it.

The exhibitor reserves the right to cancel and receive a 100 percent refund of this deposit. Written notice of such cancellation must be received by the Society within 45 days after the mailing of the 1998 Exhibitor Kit. We anticipate a mailing date of November 1, 1997 for the Phoenix show.
You must be a business member in good standing at the time you send us your booth balance. We begin accepting dues for 1998 on September 1, 1997. Remember, you are paying your membership in September of 1997 for calendar year 1998.

As there are limited number of booths and many of them were reserved on site, it is essential that you return this form as soon as possible. Assigning the booths remaining from the Minneapolis show are strictly first come first serve and the deposit must accompany this form.

Sample booth space application at the Society of Decorative Painters Convention.

Las Vegas CREATIVE PAINTING Convention

P.O. Box 80720 • Las Vegas, NV 89180
(702) 221-8234 • **Hours: 11:00 a.m. - 6:00 p.m., <u>PACIFIC</u> TIME**

(BOOTH EXHIBIT APPLICATION AND CONTRACT)

1998 *Las Vegas*
Creative Painting Convention

Wed., Feb. 25 - Fri., Feb. 27, 1998
Tropicana Hotel/Casino - Las Vegas, Nevada

TERMS AND CONDITIONS FOR EXHIBITING:

Each 8' x 10' space is $495.00, which includes space rental, one 8' draped table, two chairs, and one ID sign. (A limited number of 10' x 10' spaces are available at $525.00 each. Any additional furnishings needed for booths may be rented from the show decorator. Decorator and drayage info will be sent to each exhibitor prior to the show.

Sub-leasing is NOT allowed. Exhibitors my NOT assign or sublet any part of their space without written consent of the show Chairman. Any person or firm not exhibiting is prohibited from soliciting business in any part of the convention site. Creative Painting reserves the right to refuse service to any person or firm.

To cancel, notice must be sent in writing to the Convention Director. Prior to April 30, 1997, the cancellation fee is $100 per booth. From May 1 - Oct. 31, cancellation charge is 50% of total booth rental. After Oct. 31, 1997, 10% of space rental is refundable on cancellations. In the event of cancellation of show, only the portion of fee required to cover expenses will be retained.

Creative Painting, the show decorator, and the Tropicana Hotel will not be responsible for any loss, damage, or injury that may occur to any exhibitor, their representatives or property, before, during, or after show hours. Exhibitors should insure themselves against such claims, and by signature on application release the Tropicana Hotel and Creative Painting from any and all liability. Creative Painting will provide security for the exhibit area from set-up day through show closing, however, exhibitors should not leave booths unattended during show hours, and displays must remain intact until show closes.

All merchandise and exhibits must conform to Clark County fire codes and ordinances, and any regulations of the Tropicana Hotel.

Exhibitor agrees to abide by official show rules and regulations as set forth by the Convention Director

Children under age 16 will NOT be admitted to the exhibit hall.

Exhibitors are each responsible for the collection and payment of any sales tax, and obtaining of licences or permits which may be required by Clark County, Nevada.

# of 8' x 10' Booths	_____	@ $495 each, if paid IN FULL in advance
		OR pay $260 deposit with application and balance of $260 by Oct. 31, 1997 ($520 total)**
# of 10' x 10' Booths	_____	@ $525 each, if paid IN FULL in advance
		OR pay $275 deposit with application and balance of $275 by Oct. 31, 1997 ($550 total)**
		[Note: There are a limited number of 10 x 10's, all along the east wall of the exhibit hall.]
8 ft. table display	_____	@ $295 each; (must be paid in full with application)

**Space not paid for in full by Oct. 31, 1997 is subject to re-assignment to another exhibitor without notice or deposit refund.

** Note: Discounted prices apply ONLY if payment is made IN FULL at time of application.

You should call and check booth availability before mailing. Space is limited, and usually sold out long before show dates.

SET-UP: Tue., Feb. 24   SHOW DATES: Wed., Feb. 25 (9 - 6); Thu., Feb. 26 (9 - 6); Fri., Feb. 27 (9 - 3)

Company Name _____
Contact Person _____
Address _____
City_____ State _____ Zip _____
Area Code & Phone_____
 Fax _____
 E-mail_____

SIGNATURE_____

By signature at left, exhibitor agrees to all terms and conditions.
Booth location preference (if any):
Please locate booth near:_____
Do not locate booth near:_____

Date_____ Pmt _____
Payment receipt acknowledged by: _____
booth number(s) assigned: _____
Accepted as exhibitor by:_____

PLEASE RETURN THIS CONTRACT WITH PAYMENT TO: Creative Painting, P.O. Box 80720, Las Vegas, NV 89180.
A signed copy of this contract will be sent as confirmation upon acceptance. Booth numbers will be assigned as soon as possible.

(FOR ANSWERS TO ANY QUESTIONS ABOUT THE LAS VEGAS CONVENTION, CALL JAY SHARP AT CREATIVE PAINTING, (702) 221-8234, 11 a.m. - 6 p.m. PACIFIC TIME)

Sample Las Vegas Creative Painting Convention booth exhibitor application.

Linda Pinion: The Ultimate Show Girl

Some painters have no desire to teach or own a shop, but still want to use their skills to generate income. Linda Pinion chose the path of painting in quantity and selling at shows. She began selling her painted wooden ornaments at a large craft show in Arkansas before the show was "large" and craft shows were a way of life for many artists. From the beginning, Linda's creative mind seemed to be exactly in tune with what people would buy. Her line of painted items changed each year, echoing what was popular, while staying unique and affordable for her loyal customers. She virtually sold out at each show.

At one time Linda occupied four booth spaces at the largest show in the area. To produce the amount of merchandise needed, she painted continually between shows. She designed many of her own wood pieces and was fortunate to have a husband who was skilled with a saw and cut out most of the wood. She produces many of the smaller designs in quantity but includes a number of one-of-a-kind items to satisfy customers who want something unique.

Because of the large number of shows, craft malls and other venues for selling painted merchandise, it is more difficult to earn a living at shows than it once was. It can still be done, but it requires originality, knowledge of the marketplace and lots of hard work. ✌

Trade magazines and newspapers will have listings of shows. Consignment shops and craft malls sometimes have newspapers and flyers advertising upcoming shows. Magazines designed to advertise and sell finished crafts usually publish listings of shows.

Which Show Is Best for You?

After you have done your research and know what types of shows are available in your area, it's time to give serious thought to exactly which type of show is best for you. Beginning with a one-day, close-to-home show is definitely the best way to start, whether it's a show you organize yourself or one where you rent booth space. If you decide on a show you organize yourself, count on doing a lot of planning beforehand. Then comes the actual preparation and, finally, the show.

If you decide on an organized show, begin by requesting an application form, sometimes called a prospectus. It will list all of the information you need to submit. You might want to get applications for several different shows. This will give you an overview of booth fees, percentages and available dates. If you are not accepted by your first choice, you will have other options. Show sponsors usually notify you of acceptance well in advance of the sale, so you will have adequate time to prepare.

How Much Merchandise Do I Need?

The next and equally important thing to consider is whether or not you can have enough merchandise ready to make your sale interesting, to inspire people to buy and to make enough money to justify your time and effort. There is no way to set exact numbers, but you need enough merchandise to form a pleasing display and to make a statement about what you do. A booth with only half a dozen pieces gives the impression it has been picked over and not much is left. One consignment shop I remember usually had a large display of handmade pottery. When they received a new supply, it sold rapidly. As the inventory got smaller, even though the pieces were well done, creative and reasonably priced, customers seemed to be less interested.

Expenses

Another determining factor in the "how much product" equation is the amount of expenses incurred in doing a show over and above the cost of finished products. You need to consider what you will spend on postage, invitations and other expenses in promoting a home show. If you participate in an organized show, add up entry fees, commissions, gas, food, lodging and other out-of-pocket expenses. What you hope to clear at a sale depends on your needs and expectations. Some people are very happy if they clear $100, because it is more than they had before the show. Others want to make enough so they feel they have been well paid for their time and are not simply covering expenses without profit. If you spend $200 on a booth, you will need to have, as a bare minimum, $1,000 worth of merchandise. Your raw materials and supplies can represent 20 to 40 percent of the selling price, and it is highly unlikely you will sell everything you take. This cuts your profit margin down considerably.

Walking through a very large four-day craft show, I overheard an exhibitor talking to a friend. He said the promoter of the show wouldn't even let you in if you didn't have at least $2,000 worth of merchandise. I wondered why anyone with less would even *want* to do a four-day show where booth fees and expenses for food and lodging would eat up profits so quickly.

Take a critical look at all the costs you will incur, plus the initial investment in supplies. Balance this against the total of your merchandise to weigh the profit margin you can realistically hope for.

It's a good idea to have a few economically priced items. Most shoppers will buy your work priced at $5 or $10 without thinking twice, but when it comes to high dollar pieces, they will be more selective. The small items can be your bread and butter—the sales that pay your expenses at each show—while the more expensive pieces are the profit makers.

Time to Produce

When painting for shows, it is essential to use time as productively as possible. When you are doing several pieces of the same item, paint in multiples, work on four to six or more at a time. Organize your work space so everything you need for each painting session is within easy reach. Set aside one day to do antiquing and finishing. If your pieces are decorated with Spanish moss, flowers, ribbon wire or other accessories, do as much of it at the same time as possible. It wastes time to move your paints aside, heat the glue gun and rummage through supplies looking for the right add-on for just one surface.

Factors to consider in determining the amount of merchandise you need for a financially successful show

The following examples are only meant to give you profit/loss ratio comparisons. They are not figures to suggest ideal goals to set, only guidelines of things to consider. They do not include the unforeseen expenses that sometimes occur. Remember, too, the chances of selling *everything* you take to a show are very slim, but your expenses remain the same whether you sell out or not. Thus, it is even possible to have a loss rather than a profit on the bottom line.

These expenses are possibly higher than you will incur, and you can find many creative ways to cut back the cost of each individual element.

HOME SHOW

Dollar sales value of total inventory $2,000
Cost of materials, based on 40 percent total inventory 800
Advertising—postage, printing, flyers, etc. 150
Refreshments 50
Tags, ticket books and general supplies 20
Miscellaneous 20
Total expenses 1,040 1,040
Net profit—if you sell *all* your merchandise $960

TWO-DAY OUT-OF-TOWN CRAFT SHOW

Dollar sales value of total inventory $4,000
Cost of materials, based on 40 percent of total inventory 1,600
Booth fee/commission 300
Transportation 150
Meals and lodging (two days, two nights) 200
Equipment (lights, tablecloths, display boards, etc.) 200
Tags, ticket books, booth supplies 40
Miscellaneous 25
....2,515 2,515
Net profit—if you sell *all* your merchandise $1,485

Buying Supplies

It is a good time to talk about the costs of raw materials. In any business, maintaining low production costs is one of the keys to success. You need to purchase raw materials as economically as possible. One good way to do this is to buy wholesale from manufacturers and distributors. It cuts your costs by almost half and will increase your profit considerably. Unfortunately, this isn't always possible, because certain criteria must be met.

Wholesalers require that buyers have a resale tax number, because they are selling to the end user, and the end user is the only one required to collect and pay sales tax. Acquiring a tax certificate is easier in some states than in others. Having a tax number also is useful when you buy supplies retail. If you carry it with you or have it on file where you purchase supplies, you will not be required to pay sales tax. (For more tax information see Chapter 7.)

Manufacturers and distributors usually have a minimum dollar amount per purchase. Often, this leads the purchaser into overbuying in order to meet the minimum required. This is a trap you must avoid. There are no savings if you buy more product than you use. Buying wholesale may be an avenue to consider only after you know your business will be a moneymaker.

Quality Materials

Because a great deal of decorative painting is done on wood, finding a source for wood can be a major stumbling block in becoming a profitable business. Some painters are skilled enough to cut their own wood, while others are lucky enough to have a family member who can do it. If you don't fall into either group, you are left to buy ready-made wood or find a person who can produce the pieces for you. A good woodcutter can save you a great deal of preparation time if the wood piece is well made and properly sanded. Using valuable painting time to prepare poor quality painting surfaces is never a savings. Cost of the painting surface and preparation time are major factors in how profitable your business will be.

Retail Discounts

Some large craft chains give discounts to professional crafters. Usually you need to register at the store or carry a special discount card. Remember to compare prices. A 10 percent discount isn't a good deal if the merchandise is 20 percent higher than the competition's.

Other Bargain Sources

Some painters find most of their painting surfaces at tag sales, thrift stores and antiques shops. One very successful painter uses the summer months to scour the countryside looking for bargains she can turn into wonderful pieces of painted furniture. She considers shopping to be her summer job and uses the time to purchase, plan and prepare for the fall shows. To buy this way, you need money to invest that does not have to be recouped immediately. You also have to be creative enough to see the possibilities in a piece that may not have a lot of appeal at the time of purchase, and you will need storage space, but this type of buying can certainly supply you with unusual painting surfaces at bargain prices.

If you don't want to spend the time doing the things mentioned above, at least try to buy supplies when they are on sale. Remember that whatever you save on supplies shows up at the other end as profit.

Pricing Your Merchandise

To many painters and crafters, setting the price of merchandise is the most difficult part of selling. Prices must be reasonable enough to attract buyers, yet high enough to make as much profit as possible. It's a fine line, and an error either way can seriously affect the end result. Snob appeal will only go so far. Of course, you want to make as much as possible, but if you price yourself out of the market, you won't make anything, and you will end up with merchandise that is shopworn and out-of-date.

Most novices tend to price their items too low. They think any sale is better than none, and they are afraid of looking overpriced when compared to the competition. But if you only break even or lose money, it will cease to be fun and you will lose interest. Besides, underpricing your work may make buyers think that if you don't value your own work, maybe it isn't worth buying. So underpricing can be as bad as overpricing.

There are pricing formulas that say "x times the cost of raw materials" or "cost of raw materials plus x times y," with x representing the hours spent and y being a pay-per-hour rate. These formulas don't always work as well as you would imagine. Some people are great shoppers and fast painters, which keeps the cost of raw materials low as well as the painting time. Other people buy at retail or do intricate, time-consuming work, so their money and time investments are high.

The formula that seems to work best is to consider the cost of raw materials, the overhead involved, any selling costs and what is necessary to pay yourself adequately for your time. Set an hourly wage that you feel is fair. This is up to you and will depend on your skill level and experience. Regardless, add it to your other expenses. You may discover that the type of painting you do is so expensive that selling it would be difficult. You may need to look elsewhere for income.

Inventory Lists

Make an inventory list of all of your merchandise before you begin to pack for a show. An accurate list will make it easier to keep track of sales. Many exhibitors assign a number to each piece as they price it then record the piece on the list with the same number and a brief description, so there are two ways to identify each item.

Put price tags on the items at the same time you list them in your inventory. This eliminates the need to handle each piece twice.

Price Tags

Price tags should be large enough to read, but not so large that they detract from the overall look of your booth or table. I prefer hangtags to stickers. They can be attached to the back of a painting and still be visible from the front. Do not stick a price tag on a beautifully finished surface. It can leave a sticky residue or pull paint off when it is removed, and it's easy to scratch or damage the surface when you try to remove it. Why gamble with your artwork? Attach the price tag to the bottom or back of the merchandise, place it on the table next to the item or tape it beside the piece on the display board.

Price tags can carry more information than the cost of the item. They can be a good form of advertising. It never hurts to keep your name in front of the customer. Smart exhibitors list not only the price, but also their name and address or phone number so buyers can get in touch with them again. With readily available rubber stamps, stickers and scissors that make fancy edges, there is no excuse for ho-hum price tags.

Making Your Own Price Tags

If you make hangtags on your computer, design them so they fold over like a book. You can put your logo on the front and your name, address and phone number on the back, leaving the inside for the price. If you use price stickers on your hangtags, you can remove only the sticker at the time of sale. This leaves the buyer with a tag that tells how to reach you.

My tag can be easily changed to fit different occasions. I have "Paintings by Dorothy" on the front, and the word "Paintings" can be quickly changed to "Florals" or "Designs." I then print them on pastel or country-style paper, use pastel ribbon or jute twine rather than gold cord for hanging, and the look of the tag changes to suit the occasion. The same basic idea can be used for tags made with rubber stamps.

Speaking of identifying yourself, it is money well spent to have business cards printed and available for customers. Use the same logo on business cards and price tags. Let customers know who you are and make yourself memorable. They can't come back if they can't find you!

Packing Your Artwork

With all of the fun behind you—shopping, painting and admiring your finished work—it's time to get down to the business of packing, loading, transporting, unpacking and setting up a booth. (Another bonus in home shows is that none of this is necessary.)

Before attempting to pack anything, be sure your painted pieces are *completely* and *absolutely* dry. One of the worst things that can happen is to have wrapping materials stick to the painted surfaces of your artwork. I prefer bubble wrap because it is very good protection, and it is lint free, reusable and doesn't make a mess. Old blankets and quilts also make good packing material, but they are too bulky for small items. Unused newsprint paper is another choice. Printed newspapers are messy. The ink rubs off on you and your artwork. Styrofoam "peanuts" are a mess to deal with in a booth. Whatever your choice, be absolutely sure your artwork is well protected. You have spent too much time and money to become careless at this point. Scratched and damaged pieces won't sell.

Packing boxes of equal size and shape with lids that lift off are wonderful because they stack well and can be opened and closed easily. Label boxes so you know where everything is. It's very unprofessional to have to dig through five or six boxes in the middle of a show to look for items you need.

Pack the car in a logical way so you can get to the things you need first without unpacking the entire car. The last things you should pack are the first things you'll need to use—your tool box and the supplies necessary for setting up the booth and putting up your displays. It's much easier to get the booth set up if you don't have to step around and crawl over boxes of merchandise. If at all possible, leave the merchandise in the car until you are ready to set up your display. The last things you need to unpack are the items needed at the time of sale, such as ticket books, bags, tissue paper and your cash register or cash box.

Make a list of everything you might need in your booth—tools, ticket books, stapler, paper clips, extra pens, etc. Tape your list to the box in which you carry your booth supplies. That way you always have the list handy, and you can check off the items as you pack for the show. A recommended supply list can be found on page 28.

Setting up for a Show

Creating an Attractive Display

In planning for a show, don't forget the importance of an appealing display. It's a good idea to attend a few shows or walk through craft malls to see how other artists display their painted items. Beat-up brown display boards or tables without covers can make even the best work look undesirable. You need a background that shows your merchandise at its best. Strive for a display that complements what you do without overpowering it.

To set up for a show, the first thing you must know is how much space you will have and whether tables, display boards or backdrops will be provided. Some organized shows supply at least one table. Others charge a rental fee for tables and display boards. If the fee is reasonable, it may be worth the cost to have them supplied and set up. Metal folding tables, while handy, take a large vehicle to transport and are heavy to carry in and out of a showroom. There are also a great variety of display racks available, but it's best to wait until you do a few shows to decide if you need them. Find out what would work best for you and whether shows are really what you want to do before you invest a lot of money in fixtures.

If you decide to rent fixtures that are available, ask if the display boards are painted and if the tables are draped. If the answer is no to both questions, you should take paper or fabric to cover the display boards and for table skirts and toppers. Covering display boards doesn't involve much time. You can push Peg-Board hooks through paper or lightweight fabric, and it looks much nicer than plain boards. Table skirts that go all the way to the floor are a good idea because they create hidden storage for extra stock and empty boxes.

Traffic Flow

Look at the location of your booth in relation to the entry into the show. Try to imagine the likely path of the traffic flow. If possible, arrange your booth so it faces into the traffic and gives the best view to arriving customers. If you plan to allow customers inside your booth, arrange tables and display pieces to create an easy traffic flow. If a bottleneck hampers entering or leaving your booth, some customers will pass by, rather than deal with the traffic jam.

Lighting

Lighting is another important point to consider when setting up a booth. Inadequate lighting can be a serious disadvantage. It's smart to buy several spotlight type fixtures with clip-on attachments. They aren't expensive (under $10) and can make a big difference in your booth. A well-lit booth is far more inviting than one with poor lighting. If you take the lights, be sure to toss in a couple of extension cords, and pray that an electric outlet will be within reach.

Once you've done all of the things required to set up a booth and display your merchandise, the next step should be fun. The show opens, and you start to sell your artwork.

Selling Tips

Like everything else that involves sales, there are certain guidelines you need to follow. Notice that I said "guidelines," not rules. Everyone

Judy Diephouse & Lynne Deptula

Lynne and Judy's booth at the Heart of Ohio Tole Convention is always classically simple. Eye-catching cloths draw you in to the warm and inviting booth. Desk lamps draw attention to Lynne and Judy's finished work as well as their pattern packets. The booth's open feeling allows more people to view the artists' work.

Judy and Lynne are business partners. They teach around the country at several painting conventions and produce their own line of pattern packets under their business name, Distinctive Brushstrokes.

approaches selling from a different perspective. Finding the sales approach that works best for you often is a case of trial and error. There are certain no-no's, however, that apply to every sale. The worst exhibitor is the one who sits in the booth and looks totally bored with the whole thing. Well, if the exhibitor is not excited about his or her work, who will be? The best exhibitor is enthusiastic and attentive without being pushy—another one of those fine lines. People like to feel welcome, so smile, be friendly and let them know you want them to look around. Be excited about what you have to sell, be proud of it and be willing to explain its outstanding features to any customer who appears interested. Then back off slightly and let the customer browse without feeling you are following them around or pushing merchandise at them.

When a customer decides to make a purchase, be prepared to handle it with ease. Have a sales book handy in case they ask for a receipt. Keep several pens on hand for check writing. Pens disappear from a booth faster than merchandise sometimes. Invest in a box of inexpensive pens so you will always have one available.

If you are recording sales in a notebook, do it at the time of the sale, so you don't forget. Some vendors remove the price tag with the merchandise number on it and stick it in the notebook. You should also have a supply of change. Don't forget to add the sales tax, if it isn't already factored into the selling price. An inexpensive cash register can keep track of sales, divide merchandise into categories and figure sales tax and change. If you find that you enjoy selling, investing in a cash register certainly makes record keeping easier. Sales are handled faster and change figured with fewer mistakes, so it's an investment that pays for itself in a short period of time. A cash register also can be locked if necessary and is much more of a deterrent to thieves than a cash box. It's sad but true, theft is a problem that must be considered, so be careful how you handle cash in your booth. Don't ever keep your cash box where it would be handy or tempting to a thief. You've worked too hard to have someone walk away with your profits.

You should have tissue paper, bubble wrap or other wrapping materials handy. Wrapping painted pieces in newspaper is not a good idea because the ink can rub off onto the merchandise. It's also smart to have bags in several sizes. If at all possible, invest in new bags. Used grocery sacks are OK for flea markets but are not suitable for beautifully painted works of art.

Organizing Your Own Local Show

A few artists and craftspeople have used their experience and knowledge to organize their own large shows. Note that I used the words "experience" and "knowledge." Organizing a local show is rarely an option if you have never been involved in shows and don't have a working knowledge of management and/or promotion. But it can be done. One woman started what has become one of the largest, best attended shows in our area, because she and a few friends wanted to sell their arts and crafts. The show grew each year until she finally had to move it to the local fairgrounds. She schedules three shows each year. The fall show, which is the largest, now has seven buildings filled with exhibitors. The winter and spring shows are slightly smaller. She has even branched out and is doing shows in other cities. That kind of success is rare, but it can happen.

Selling at shows is not for everyone. Some people seem to thrive on the show circuit and achieve great success, both financially and personally, while others feel it is far too much work or not financially rewarding enough, or they simply don't like dealing with the public. But it's only one of the ways to make money with your decorative painting. Before you make up your mind, let's look at a few of the other options.

If you sell your artwork at shows, it helps to have the following basic supplies packed in a box so you don't have to make a last-minute scramble to gather tools. I tape or write the list on the lid so I can check to be sure I haven't "borrowed" anything and not put it back.

TOOLBOX SUPPLIES

- Hammer
- Nails in assorted sizes
- Screwdrivers (regular and Phillips)
- Pliers
- Wire (fine and heavy gauge)
- Wirecutters
- Staple gun and staples
- Surge protector 6-way outlet
- Heavy-duty 3-prong extension cord
- Masking tape
- Adhesive Velcro hook-and-loop strips
- Dust cloth
- Packing tape
- Packing knife
- Thumbtacks or pushpins

BOOTH SUPPLIES

- Pens
- Paper clips
- Cellophane tape
- Stapler and staples
- Business cards
- Envelopes
- Publicity materials (flyers, publication lists, etc.)
- Business cards
- Rubber bands
- Black marker and permanent pen
- Blank index cards
- Small spiral notebook
- Pins (straight and safety)
- Price tags and/or stickers
- Hole puncher
- Change (coins and small denomination bills)
- Bank bag

OPTIONAL

- Peg-Board hooks
- Tape measure or ruler
- Ticket books
- Cash box or cash register and extra cash register tapes
- Deposit stamp for checks and stamp pad, if needed
- Lights and extra bulbs
- Extension cord for each light
- Drill and assorted drill bits
- Sacks and tissue paper

CHAPTER THREE

Other Ways to Sell Your Decorative Painting

IF THE RIGORS OF SELLING at shows seem too much for you, you will want to consider other ways of marketing your painted pieces. Let's look at some other options.

Selling to Friends and Family

The best part of selling directly to friends, family, neighbors and co-workers is that sales just seem to happen. Acquaintances see what you have painted and ask if you would consider selling that item or painting another one like it. It can be as simple as that. Suddenly, you are in business. Another advantage is that sales are generally handled directly, thus eliminating any middleman, situations, such as craft malls and selling commissions, that eat into profits.

The downside is you will be tempted to sell the work for less than it is worth. That attitude is sweet, but if you aren't getting a fair price for your work, you will soon tire of selling at a loss. It also puts the buyer at a disadvantage. When I first began to sell my work, a good friend asked me to do some pieces for her. Since she was such a good friend, I charged her basically what the materials cost, with nothing included for my time. When she realized what I had done, she mentioned a problem I had never considered. She said if I didn't charge a fair price, she wouldn't be comfortable asking me to do more art in the future. We would both miss a great opportunity—hers to enjoy my work and mine to make a sale. So, be fair to everyone when you price your painted pieces. Selling for too little can be a problem for the buyer as well as the seller.

The other problem in selling to friends and relatives is that frequently they have no concept of what is involved in producing a beautifully painted piece of art. They might consider the cost of the raw materials, but they rarely consider the amount of time and money spent developing the skills to produce it. Try not to get caught off guard without a fair price for your work in mind. Know what your art is worth. It gives you a bargaining position and an air of professionalism. Next, it becomes your job to gently educate the friend or relative. If they ask for a freebie, tell them how pleased you are they like your work. Then briefly explain what high-quality, sometimes expensive, materials you use, how much work it takes to prepare each surface and how long you have worked to achieve the ability to paint well enough to create these works of art. Keep your explanation brief and lighthearted, but make it clear you can't afford giveaways. Then tell them the price without any apology.

If friends or relatives admire an expensive item, you might offer to paint something similar but less costly. If you want to and can afford to offer a discount, explain that you want to give them a special price because of your relationship. Request that it be an agreement between the two of you, because you can't afford to do it for everyone. You might also ask them to recommend you to their friends or co-workers. It then becomes a win-win situation: Buyers feel they are getting preferential treatment, and you make a fair profit and possibly gain new markets for your work.

Selling to Co-Workers

If you work in an office, school or any area where you have co-workers, and there are no rules about selling in the business area, it can become a wonderful customer base. Office workers and teachers have limited shopping time, so they are usually happy to have the opportunity to buy unique items at work. But don't overdo it. Let people know what you do and what is available, but don't be pushy. Nobody likes to be constantly inundated with merchandise or badgered into spending money.

Even if you don't work in an office or school, you can sell your work through friends who do. One painter has several friends who are teachers. Just before each major holiday, she paints an assortment of jewelry with the holiday theme, attaches them to attractive cards, prices and arranges them in pretty baskets and lets her friends take them to the schools where they teach. She sells everything she sends! Many teachers love special-occasion jewelry and eagerly await her baskets. She also paints special things for the friends who handle the sales, so they know she appreciates their help.

Ask if you can display your work at your favorite hair or nail salon. Be sure to leave a supply of your business cards so interested patrons can contact you for custom work.

In-Home Parties

This type of show differs from the private home show because it is formatted much like a Tupperware party. The salesperson acts as an agent for several craftspeople and artists. She schedules parties, where guests can see samples of the merchandise and place orders for delivery at a later date. This is not a widely available avenue and depends solely on finding an agent interested in promoting and sponsoring this idea. Usually it is someone who has done other types of home parties, so they understand how to conduct the party. They may be acquainted with several artists and/or have artwork or crafts they produce, giving them a steady source of suppliers. The major problem with this type of sale is it only works as well as the salesperson presenting it does. If you find someone whose selling abilities and "showmanship" are outstanding, you can make very good money with this idea. Unfortunately, this option is not as popular and as available as other methods of selling.

Craft Malls

Because malls usually include more crafters than painters, in this segment we will refer to the booth holders as crafters rather than painters or artists, but the same rules apply.

Craft malls furnish a way to have your work before the buying public without spending your time attending a booth or shop. You only need to go in at specified times to restock or rearrange your merchandise. Most people who sell their work at craft malls live nearby, but if mall selling is successful, you may want to display your work in other areas. Most malls will arrange and restock for out-of-town booth holders.

If you decide to venture into malls, find one or more to consider, then walk through the mall to get the overall feeling of how it looks. Ask yourself the following questions:

- Is it the atmosphere you want?
- Does it have an air of professionalism?
- Is it well maintained?
- Does it have good lighting?
- Is the booth space adequate to showcase your work?
- Is the work of the other crafters of the quality and in the price range that fits with yours?

All of these questions will affect your sales. If you are happy with the answers to these questions, you are ready to approach the managers of the mall. Ask them to explain how the mall operates. Methods of operation can vary greatly. Even malls with the same owners may charge higher booth fees in different locations because their expenses are higher. Some malls charge only the monthly rent on the booth. Others charge rent plus a percentage of your sales. Look at booth sizes and ask the cost of each size. Be sure to ask if a lease is required and, if so, for how long.

If they take credit cards, it can greatly increase sales, but find out if that percentage will be deducted from your sales.

Some locations are seasonal. Ask if they are open year round and what hours they are open. Most seasonal locations are near tourist attractions, so it is possible to have better sales, even with a shorter selling season, because of the heavy traffic in the peak season.

Advertising and special promotions should also be considered. Some malls even advertise on a national level. Others have demonstrations or special events to attract customers.

Malls usually limit the number of crafters in each category. For example, they will only handle a certain number of decorative painters or woodworkers. This makes the store more interesting and helps to limit competition within the mall. The mall management will expect to see samples of your work. Some like to see the actual pieces, but others will accept slides and/or photographs.

ook for craft malls in your area. If none are available or you are looking for a larger market, contact the following malls for booth information and a list of locations. Many chains limit their locations to specific areas, so you may need to look for a chain closer to you. The following chains are expanding and promote their stores at national craft markets, such as the Association of Crafts and Creative Industries and Hobby Industry Association. Some of the chains also sponsor weekend craft shows in several locations and have galleries on the Internet.

Coomers Craft Mall
(888) 362-7238

Coomers Global Gallery
http://www.coomers.com

Country Sampler Store
311 N. 2nd St., St. Charles, IL 60174
(630) 377-8128

Crafters' Showcase
(414) 250-0400
(414) 327-0400
(414) 376-0400

You should also ask how payment for your sold work will be handled. Ask when and how often crafters are paid. If you feel the need to speak to other booth holders about how the mall is doing or how promptly they are paid, don't hesitate to request the names of people who have their work there. Most mall owners are happy to supply references, and some even include comments from booth holders in their information packets.

Ask about restocking your display area. Often, certain hours are set aside for restocking so that booths are not in a state of disarray while shoppers are in the store. Other stores will allow restocking at the booth holder's convenience. Some malls may require displays to be changed and refreshed at regular intervals. Seasonal merchandise should always be removed or reduced in price when the prime selling time has passed.

Some malls are similar to chain stores, because they have multiple locations. Some even offer franchise operations. These stores frequently have booth holders from other parts of the country. The mall operators will stock the booths of out-of-town crafters and replenish inventory. Some malls photograph your completed booth display and send the picture to you to be sure they arranged it to your satisfaction.

If you decide to use a mall away from your area, consider the cost of delivering your merchandise. If you plan to drive there, factor in travel expenses and time spent. If you ship the merchandise, make allowances for freight costs.

Craft Mall Advantages and Disadvantages

With all of this information, you are now ready to evaluate the pros and cons of craft mall selling. The biggest advantages are more exposure and that you do not have to be on site to sell your painted works. This allows you more time to paint and produce merchandise to sell. You do need to consider, however, how high you will need to price your work to give you a satisfactory profit margin after paying the booth fee and/or commission. Will your work still be priced competitively? If the answers to these questions satisfy you, a mall may be the answer to your marketing needs.

Selling Through Consignment, Co-ops and Sales Representatives

Consignments

Some decorative painters have found success and financial rewards selling through retail stores. There are several ways to enter this market. The first one is simply to approach a local shop about carrying your merchandise. Some shop owners are willing to buy directly from artists who can supply products suitable for their type of store, but you must be willing to offer a discount of at least 40 percent.

Selling outright is a great deal better than selling on consignment, because you know for sure the merchandise is sold and won't be returned to you months later, possibly shopworn and out-of-date. Therefore, selling your artwork yourself at a lower price may be a wise decision to make.

Selling on consignment works for some people, but it is not for everyone. If you are not careful about selecting a shop, your beautifully painted pieces can get damaged and shopworn very quickly. Some consignment shops simply do not take proper care of the merchandise because they have no actual investment in it. Never decide to put your art in a shop solely because they are willing to take it on consignment. Check the store to be sure they have adequate display space, that consignments are handled carefully on a professional level and they have a large enough customer base to support good sales. If your painted pieces just sit on the shelf, no one profits. You would be wise to ask other consignors if they are happy with how the store is run and if they are being paid as agreed.

Commissions vary from store to store, but expect to pay at least 35 percent of the selling price in commission. Some shops charge as much as 50 percent. It is difficult, if not impossible, to pay the overhead on a store with only a 35 percent profit margin. My experience as a partner in a very successful consignment shop was a real eye opener as to how much it costs to run a store. Some months it took almost all the profits just to pay rent and utilities. Advertising is very costly. We eventually added antiques and ready-made gifts to supplement our consignment stock. They could carry a higher mark-up, and that sometimes made the difference in making a profit and just meeting expenses. In other words, don't think shop owners are taking advantage of you by asking a higher commission on consignment sales. They only want to run a profitable business, and that is an advantage for you as well as the store.

Co-ops

Co-ops are less popular now than they were in past years for several reasons. People don't want to take the time to be part of a co-op. Co-ops take more organization and time than it appears at first glance. Someone needs to coordinate working hours, handle necessary bookwork and take care of the problems occurring in any retail space. Co-ops have to pay rent, utilities and insurance, and someone has to make sure these areas are covered. Unless you can find enough space at a low rent, it is not always easy to meet expenses. Many co-ops that are set up for profit are multipurpose, so members can use their space as a studio or classroom as well as for display and sales. This seems to work well because artists are available to serve customers while accomplishing other things, thus putting their time at the co-op to good use.

I know several co-ops that are doing well as civic-based endeavors. However, the rent is very low and the profits don't need to be large enough to support the participants. One such place is a small coffee and soup shop established to support art programs for children. It does well because the building is rent free and the help is volunteer. The participants can do their civic volunteering to support the arts and, at the same time, have the opportunity to display and sell their work.

Sales Representatives

Selling through sales representatives is another way to get your art into the marketplace, but, like selling at gift markets, it is only a viable option for painters who want to do production work. Most sales representatives are not interested in one-of-a-kind pieces of art but want a line of products they know are available for immediate shipping and in quantities to satisfy retail merchants. If you deal with reps, be prepared to pay at least a 15 percent commission, which must be added to the discount you are offering as a wholesaler. Also be aware that most reps don't take on a product and run with it. You need to contact them at regular intervals to make sure your line stays current in their minds and in their catalogs. Using sales reps usually is not a successful endeavor for painters.

Selling Wholesale Through Gift Markets

If you plan to sell your painted work wholesale, you must be able to mass produce a line of products. That requires dedication and organization. One painter took a line of painted accessories to a wholesale gift market and was so successful that she ended up almost having a nervous breakdown. She came home with many orders. Unfortunately, she was not prepared for this kind of success and didn't even have the wood pieces cut. Because she couldn't produce the work alone and didn't have the resources to hire painters, she ended up missing most of her deadlines, shipping late and dealing with disappointed, irate customers. If invoices were not paid on time, she didn't have enough capital to pay her helpers, and the problems multiplied in size and number.

If you think you want to try entering the wholesale marketplace, you must be committed and well prepared. It is expensive to have a booth at an established gift market, and it is absolutely essential to be prepared for success and have the resources and personnel you need. Also, remember

The following catalogs and magazines are devoted primarily to selling the work of crafters who advertise in the publication. They vary in content slightly, but their main focus is the same. Some carry decorating features, some include projects with instructions and some include patterns. Look for them on your newsstand, and if you are interested, call or write for advertising rates and/or subscription information.

Country Sampler
P.O. Box 228, St. Charles, IL 61074
(708) 377-8399

Better Homes and Gardens Craft Showcase
P.O. Box 37228, Boone, IA 50010
(800) 688-6611

Folkart Treasures Country Marketplace
P.O. Box 1823, Sioux City, IA 51102
(800) 398-5025

that most retail merchants will at least double your wholesale price, so be realistic about what your painted pieces are worth.

Direct Mail: Catalogs and Magazines

The first thing you should know is that the cost of advertising your work in catalogs and/or magazines is quite high. Advertising is expensive in publications with good circulation. And there is an old saying, "It doesn't pay to advertise just once, because it takes repeated exposure to reap large benefits." There is a great deal of truth in that adage.

There are a number of publications that specifically sell unique pieces of craft work, and many of their advertisers have had good results. Others have reported only minimal success. If you decide to try this method of selling, you must be able to meet the demands of a good response. You should also be realistic about expectations and not be overloaded or over-extended with stock. The majority of people who use this method of selling report they were definitely not swamped with orders. Most stated that they recouped the cost of the ad, but that was about all. Some stated that they received a number of requests for their catalog, and others made contacts for wholesaling their finished work or packets. Anyone will tell you that repetitive advertising is more effective. Running a single advertisement rarely generates a huge response.

If selling finished artwork is your goal, you may have to experiment to find the right niche for your work. To be financially successful, and many painters are, you will probably have to specialize in pieces that are not time-consuming to produce. Simple designs with charm and eye appeal are the secret. A few painters have developed work that can be mass produced and sold wholesale, but they paid their dues and learned from experience. They were in the marketplace long enough to discover what the public likes and were ambitious enough to produce it. If painting one-of-a-kind, time-consuming pieces is what gives you personal satisfaction, and you still hope for large financial rewards, you may need to look further for a way to market your artwork.

CHAPTER FOUR

Teaching

TEACHING IS A WONDERFUL OPPORTUNITY to share your knowledge and love of decorative painting with others and get paid for doing it. At the same time, you can improve your own skills and increase your knowledge. An old Chinese proverb says "To teach is to learn twice," and anyone who has taught painting will tell you it's true. Teaching reinforces and crystallizes what you know, and it's also a great way to stimulate your enthusiasm and stoke the fires of creativity. Students are exciting. They often take your ideas and expand them, which in turn inspires your imagination. Feedback from students can be your best source of inspiration.

Am I Ready?

You may wonder how you will know if you have the knowledge and skills to teach. The easiest answer seems to be that if someone asks you to teach them to do something, they obviously think you have knowledge to share and you know more than they do. Begin by teaching that person what they ask for. You will be surprised at how much you know and can share. Many successful teachers started by teaching a friend or neighbor at their kitchen table and now have gone on to teach nationally and even internationally. To stay ahead of students, you will have to increase your skills and knowledge so it will be a growth experience for both of you.

A shop owner or craft store manager who asks you to teach obviously thinks you paint well and are knowledgeable enough to do it. If you doubt your own abilities, begin with a single workshop. It will let you "test the waters" without making a commitment to ongoing classes. Teaching may not be for everyone, but for most painters, it is a win-win situation.

Class Preparation

If you plan to teach, you probably have a basic understanding of what is expected from classes you have attended. The size of your class and the teaching methods used will determine what you must do to prepare for class. If the class is small, you can demonstrate on the surface to be painted. A larger class requires an easel demonstration large enough for everyone to see. Some teachers give patterns, written instructions and photographs as part of the class. Once again, that decision is up to the individual teacher. If you use photographs or color copies, it's important that the students have one source to look at that is true to color. An inaccurate copy is worse than no copy at all. If you plan to expand your student base and eventually have larger classes, it will pay dividends later if you are well prepared and use a professional approach at the very beginning. Poor habits are difficult to break and good ones make life easier for everyone.

Strive to be the best teacher you can be. Go to class well prepared. If possible, have your supplies set up before class time. If you plan to pass out patterns and photographs, have them organized and ready. Allow your students to arrive early, so they can be ready to paint when class begins.

Start the class on time. If you fall into a habit of starting late, the students will arrive later and later. You will lose valuable class time that should be spent on instruction and painting. From the beginning, let the students know that class begins promptly at the time set, and they should be in their seats and ready to paint.

If possible, finish the class in the same professional manner. If you let them know they can paint past the end of class, they will stay longer each time. Then you are giving away your time and establishing a bad teaching habit. If you progress to teaching in a shop or at a convention or seminar, you will be expected to cover the material and end the class on time, so begin early to build a teaching foundation that will not have to be repaired and altered.

Teaching Methods

The most popular method of teaching, probably because it is the most successful, is to demonstrate and explain each step so the students understand it, then allow them time to complete that step. Do not cover too much at one time or they won't absorb all of it. It sometimes helps if you can carry the project around the room occasionally so they can look at it closely to see exactly how it should look.

Many teachers like to demonstrate a step, then circulate around the room to see if each student understands and can do it. They offer individual help if needed, even demonstrating close up for students who need it. If you use this method, try to move fast enough so you are back at the easel in time to do the next step.

Allow the class ample time to complete each step, but don't move so slowly that they get bored. Hitting a happy medium between the fastest painter and the slowest one in a class can be tricky. You must strive to keep the class moving at a pace that suits the majority of students. A beginning class is always taught at a slower pace than an advanced class. Beginners, who are just developing their skills and trying to absorb information at the same time, need more time and repetition to allow them to achieve success. Advanced students have already reached a higher skill level and have knowledge of the basic concepts of painting, so the class can go at a faster pace. Remember, however, advanced students may be taking your class because you offer a technique that is new to them. Don't leave out any details that set your work apart from that of other teachers.

Try to maintain a pleasant, upbeat atmosphere in your classes. Be friendly and patient. Most students are there for fun as well as to learn to paint. They want to escape from the pressures and problems in their lives. Make your criticisms gently and constructively. Compliment what is good about their work before telling them what is wrong. People everywhere respond well to sincere praise.

Students will grow in their abilities much faster if they feel confident. It is your job not only to teach them the basics of painting, but also to instill the confidence in them to try new things. They will also need confidence to practice when you are not there to show them each and every brushstroke to make. Be honest with your flattery but willing to point out mistakes and explain ways to correct them.

To be a successful teacher, you must continue to grow in knowledge and painting experience. It's fine to introduce friends and neighbors to decorative painting while you have limited skills and a willing, open attitude about sharing, but to become a professional you need much more. You need a great deal of knowledge about your style of painting and the ability to communicate how to do it. If you can't explain it clearly, your students will not be able to do it. Being unclear or unsure about a technique can mean disaster in the classroom.

Communication means a give and take of information. You must be able to explain your technique, but you also must listen to your students and sincerely want to understand and answer their questions. You need patience as well as a deep desire to share your knowledge. And you need enthusiasm and a positive attitude. The beginning student's desire to paint is usually coupled with a need for recreation and the quest to find something satisfying as well as productive. Encourage students to succeed. Do all you can to make the class a relaxing, positive, productive experience. Happy, successful students are your best advertising.

Continuing Your Education

Always strive to increase your own knowledge. You should never stop learning. There is always more to know. Take classes whenever possible. You will improve your skills, and it will give you renewed enthusiasm. You will return to your classes with new projects and inspiration. It also helps you as a teacher if you put yourself in the position of student occasionally to remind yourself how it feels.

Even if you do not learn a new technique or style of painting in the class, you may pick up a phrase or a way of explaining techniques to help you in your own classes. Be open to every aspect of the class, not just the project being taught. Watch how the teacher demonstrates, how students are helped, what materials are given and anything else to make you a better teacher. I still remember and use phrases from the first classes I took over twenty years ago. Listening to and learning from other teachers is a wonderful opportunity. Take advantage of it whenever you can.

Attracting Students to the Wonderful World of Painting

If you decided to obtain studio space or have access to a classroom environment, you are ready to build your student base. Then you need to expand that base and attract new students.

Sylvia Eaton: In-Home Studio

Sylvia Eaton wanted to teach people to paint, so she converted space in her basement into a classroom. She teaches seven classes a week with eight to ten students in each class. Her schedule includes classes for beginning, intermediate and advanced painters.

At first it was difficult to get supplies because many distributors refused to sell to an in-home business. Over the years, their policy changed as they realized there were fewer storefront shops and in-home teachers were creating a large demand for painting supplies.

Sylvia acknowledges her setup isn't perfect (she wishes the studio had a separate entrance and a bathroom), but it has given her the opportunity to teach for sixteen years. If you want to teach but cannot find a place to do it, look around your home. You may have unused space that can be converted to a classroom. Remember, the important things are finding the space and providing tables, chairs and good lighting. Teachers can be successful almost anywhere if they are well prepared, have interesting, challenging projects and truly love sharing their knowledge with their students. ✌

Peggy Nuttall: The Dream Studio

When there is no existing space in a home that can be converted to a teaching studio and no other place in town to teach, many painters build additions to accommodate their painting and teaching needs. While most of these are bare-bones one-room additions, a more ambitious approach cannot only provide studio space, but actually serve as a long-term investment designed to increase the value of the home. Peggy Nuttall built just such a studio.

Peggy's studio would fulfill the wildest dreams of any teacher. While it is an ideal teaching space, her addition is actually a self-contained apartment. It has a separate entrance, an equipped kitchen and a bathroom with shower. Because Peggy lives in a college town,

she felt that the self-contained studio not only would keep her studio space and private home completely separated, but also could be utilized as rental space for a student or living space for an aging parent. Having already decided to commit to a large investment, she went one step further and made it an area everyone would enjoy. The large open studio has a fireplace, built-in cabinets, lots of windows and good lighting. A small entry space and ample closets make the area very livable.

Peggy was willing to make a large investment in her business of teaching. However, she did it wisely, creating a versatile area that will continue to be a great asset even if she chooses to discontinue her classes. ᴥ

Attracting Students to Your Studio

If there are other shops or craft stores in your area, you must offer something different, and hopefully better than other teachers. You can attract students by offering unique projects, exciting workshops, special class times and anything else that sets you apart from the competition.

Strive to be the very best teacher in your area. Always be well prepared and organized when you enter the classroom. Know your material and be willing and able to impart all your information to your students. Be encouraging and helpful. Try to know and understand the people in your classes and what they need and expect from you.

You will have students who would be happy if you painted their entire picture. Don't fall into that trap. It's not fair to anyone. Students will not improve their skills, you will feel frustrated and used and you will cheat the other students in class by giving too much time and attention to one person.

On the other end of the spectrum are students who do not want you to touch their painting. With these people, you can offer to demonstrate on your teaching sample, on their palette or some other available surface, but respect their independence.

You will also find students who have a distinct style of their own. If that happens, try to work with them, not against them. Explain what you do and how it differs from theirs, but never force them into your mold. Your job is not to create clones but to impart knowledge. Instruct and encourage on an individual basis. Some of the most exciting work done in my classes has been by individuals who used my idea or technique in their own way and created a unique, original work of art. Allow your students to grow and develop as individuals.

Class Fees

How much to charge for classes is always a difficult question. First of all, if you are thinking about teaching, you have probably taken classes. What did your teacher charge? If she was well known and had an established following and years of teaching experience, it would be unrealistic to expect to be paid on her level. However, it would give you a guideline.

Class fees generally range from $4 to $15 for a two-or three-hour class.

If there are other teachers in the area, your fees should be in line with theirs. I do not recommend undercutting fees in an effort to attract students. It rarely works and simply is not ethical. If other teachers have far more experience, perhaps your fee should be slightly lower, but only because of the level of teaching expertise.

Series and On-Going Classes

If you teach classes as a series, such as a six- or eight-week set, it is wise to require a deposit of half of the series fee, with the remainder payable at the beginning or midway through the set. The deposit assures you the students will be there so you can accurately judge class size.

On-going classes should pay by the month. This puts the responsibility on the students to be there because, after all, you must be there whether they are or not and you should be paid for your time. Remember, if they take a course at a college or technical school, pay the tuition and then don't attend regularly, the school does not refund money for the missed classes. When you treat teaching as a business, your students will not be as tempted to take advantage of your gentle nature and kind heart. Some teachers choose to offer a make-up class once or twice a year so students can work on something they missed, but that is only an option, not an obligation.

Class Hours

The length of each class is a matter of choice. Most range from two to six hours. My favorite is a three-hour class. Two hours barely gives some students time to get all of their supplies ready. In three hours, you have adequate time to cover material thoroughly and still leave the students time for painting. An advantage to teaching a number of classes is you can have two in one day, a morning and an afternoon session. If you teach away from home, this saves travel setup time.

Another advantage to teaching two classes on the same day is that students may elect to stay for both classes. This works especially well if the class is not a paint-along, but one where students work on whatever they choose and the teacher circulates, giving individual instructions. A six-hour or all-day class is a good choice for workshops and for projects that need to be completed in a single painting session.

Tips for Organizing a Class

Many aspects of teaching depend on the skill level of the class. Beginner classes require a different kind of planning and preparation than advanced theory classes. Another factor to consider is where you are teaching. If you are teaching in your own studio or in a shop or studio belonging to someone else, this will affect your choice of subject matter, class time and various responsibilities. Here are some basic things that are essential to any class.

 Commitment to teaching and thorough preparation and organization are absolutely necessary.

 If you teach in a shop or studio other than your own, understand shop rules and policies. Find out exactly what is expected by the shop owner and who is responsible for everything, from ordering supplies to classroom cleanup. Good communication will prevent problems. The shop owner should tell you about teaching policies. Also bear in mind that shops need to sell product to pay the overhead. They probably want you to concentrate on projects that can be finished quickly so the students will move on to the next one. They want projects that attract new customers and painters, so theory and technique classes are not as popular as project classes with shop owners.

 Beginner classes are the most important. Beginners are the lifeblood of decorative painting. They must be encouraged and satisfied so they will continue taking classes. Plan projects that teach new skills. Use a variety of color combinations, brushstrokes and other basic skills necessary to becoming a successful painter, but choose projects that can be completed in one class so students have a continuing sense of success.

 If you teach large projects that cannot be completed in a single class session, divide the material into logical increments. For example, if you are teaching a large landscape on canvas that will take three sessions to complete, teach the sky and background trees in the first class. The second session should cover buildings and the middle ground of the canvas. Use the third class to complete the foreground and to add any small details not covered previously. On a large wood piece painted with acrylics you might apply the base coat to everything in the first class. Shading and highlights can be added in the second session. Complete the detail and antiquing in the third class. (I have found that most students have a three-

47

Gloria Perkins and Nora Blair: Storefront Studio

Gloria Perkins and Nora Blair have come up with a unique approach to answering the need for studio space. Both work full time at demanding jobs, so they could not maintain a retail shop that would be open during regular business hours. Neither wanted, nor had the space, to devote to an in-home studio, and no classrooms were available in nearby shops.

Gloria and Nora solved their problem by renting space in a small strip mall. They offer evening and Saturday classes and bring in national teachers twice a year for weekend workshops. The studio is only open during classes. They carry enough basic supplies to fulfill the needs of their students, and they make it clear that the profits from the supplies are what pays the rent and allows them to maintain the classroom space. Their students are very supportive and understand that if they buy supplies elsewhere, the studio will not be self-supporting and will possibly close.

Although they rarely see each other, Gloria and Nora share the workload equally, with one ordering supplies and the other paying the bills. Each cleans up after her own classes and each is responsible for one of the seminars by a visiting teacher. They say the secret is to find a reasonably priced, well-lit space and to carry a limited inventory of supplies. They only stock brushes, paints, canvases, easels, palettes, palette keepers and other items that support their classes. ❧

class limit on the amount of time they want to spend on a single project.)

※ Always include product information and proper care of materials in any beginner class or when you teach a new group of students. Explain anything unique about the products you use.

※ Put class policies in writing, and go over them briefly in class to be sure they are clearly understood. You should cover fees, registration, deposits, refund policies and makeup classes, if offered. Explain any shop policies that concern supplies and class surfaces.

Teaching in Your Home

If you have the space to do it, teaching in your home is a good way to begin. You don't have to make a large financial investment, your overhead is low and you can set your own hours. Another advantage is that all the money you earn is yours because you don't have to pay rent or a commission. However, on the downside, it can be difficult to get supplies because many distributors will not deal with in-home businesses. Also, your classes can infringe on your family's privacy. It can irritate your neighbors if you don't have adequate parking on your own property. It can be difficult to get students to leave when the class is over if there is no shop with a schedule or closing time to bring the class to an end. With adequate forethought and preparation you can eliminate some of the pitfalls.

First of all, make sure you are not in violation of any laws or neighborhood codes. Most areas allow home businesses if there are no regular employees, heavy advertising or signs posted, but you should call your city offices to inquire. It certainly won't be a profitable venture if you end up paying a fine for violating a city ordinance.

Parking can be the next major problem. A couple of cars once a week isn't a problem in most neighborhoods. However, six to ten cars, on several days each week, can soon create ill feelings among even the best of friends. Insist that students park in your allotted space and that they do not block your neighbors' driveways or access to the street.

Next you will need to find space to hold a class. Your kitchen table is fine for two or three students, but probably not for six or seven. Remember that painters need more space than just a place to sit. They need room for paints, palette, brushes, mediums and their painting surface. They also need adequate lighting. It doesn't have to be studio lighting, but if they can't see to paint, they will get discouraged rapidly. It is ideal if you have a room you can use solely as a studio or classroom. This keeps the students within given perimeters and away from your main living space.

You must have trash containers, a cleanup area and a rest room available. Some students think a coffee maker and/or refrigerator to store cold drinks are essential elements to any space where you spend several hours. That is up to you.

Opening Your Own Studio Away From Home

If teaching in your home is not an option, you may want to rent studio space elsewhere. Notice I used the term rent, rather than buy. Unless you are buying a space as an investment, don't risk your life savings on an untested venture. You should even give careful thought to this step if it involves signing a lease.

Think about the following questions:
- What are your long-term goals?
- Are you sure you will enjoy teaching?
- Can you get enough students to make it profitable?
- Do you want to be involved in selling supplies?

Many shops and teaching studios have opened and closed quickly because the teacher was not well prepared and didn't have a clear picture of what it takes to be successful. Maintaining a commercial studio takes commitment and sometimes very long hours to be successful. You must be willing to teach enough to generate income sufficient to pay rent, utilities and other expenses as well as paying yourself for your time. Since evening classes are often the most financially successful, you must also consider whether you are able and willing to sacrifice that time away from your family.

It is difficult, if not impossible, to maintain a separate studio profitably with only class fees to generate income. This means you will have to maintain a retail business, if only to sell supplies. All of the profitable studios I have seen earn the major portion of their income from merchandise sales, rather than class fees. If you are the sole teacher, class fees seem like 100

Memorandum

To: All Store Demonstrators/Teachers

From: Carolyn Curry -- Coordinator

Thank you for joining us at Hobby Lobby Creative Centers to do demonstrations. The rules and guidelines for demonstrating are as follows:

Demonstrations are scheduled for Monday through Saturday 12:00-2:00 PM. At this time, Sunday's are not available. You are expected to check in 15 minutes before the demonstration with that stores key person. The only exception would be if you were sent by a vendor to do demonstrations. Hobby Lobby has the option to keep your demonstration project for display purposes. A 20% store discount will be given in exchange. This discount must be used only on the day of the demonstration, before or after the demonstration is performed, and only for supplies used in the demonstration. The themes for the demonstrations are designed around current holidays. The person demonstrating must ask permission from the stores key person before taking products off the store shelves. Be certain that Hobby Lobby carries most of the supplies before being used for your demonstration. Arrive with a prepared brief description of what you will be demonstrating on a 3x5 index card. It will be announced. After you are through, go to a checkout stand to receive your payment. You will receive $8.00 per hour in cash. We only pay for two hours, unless special circumstances arise.

It is important to remember that you are representing Hobby Lobby; so please dress accordingly.

If you are unable to keep your demonstration time, please notify the store and myself immediately. Persons with repeated cancellations will be so noted and not rescheduled. The main idea of demonstrations is for our customers to see how to use our products. The customer will be looking for you.

Teachers
Teachers are give a 20% store discount. Hobby Lobby provides all classrooms for teaching purposes free of charge. Merchandise used for teaching must be purchased in advance. After teaching, please leave the classroom clean. All teachers are encouraged to book one month in advance to perform demonstrations. This is to better accommodate for the teaching schedule.

To become a new teacher you must go through myself. Please call after 9:00 pm at (918) 627-9194. I will need to see a sample of your work and references. You will be placed on the store calendar according to availability.

This is an example of a teacher's contract with Hobby Lobby.

percent profit, but it isn't profit until the bills are paid. If most of the money you take in goes to pay the bills, you will quickly lose interest in teaching.

The most natural way to increase the amount of capital coming into the studio is to sell supplies needed in the classes. Encourage your students to purchase all supplies at the studio. Let them know, without being overbearing and alienating them, that the supplies sold help you maintain a place for them to paint. Without some profit, you cannot stay open. In the beginning, carry only what is needed for the classes. Use supplies that are unique to your shop. Paint on special wood pieces that can't be found elsewhere. Use brands of paint and quality canvases that are not available at discount stores. You may want to offer a student discount. It cuts your profit, but it encourages students to buy and gives you a fast turnover.

Try to set aside the profits from supplies to purchase more merchandise. This way, your inventory will grow. If you buy cautiously, you will always have money to pay for merchandise when payment is due. Establishing good credit with your suppliers is absolutely essential.

If you make mistakes and merchandise doesn't sell, get rid of it. Reduce the price, offer a special deal with another purchase, but get it out of the way, and replace it with something that will sell. Keep your supplies current with the classes being offered.

Teaching in Shops and Craft Stores

Once you have some experience teaching in your home, you may choose to approach local shops about teaching in their stores, or they may approach you. Establish good business practices at the very beginning. Ask questions to determine what is expected of you:

- Who orders supplies?
- Who handles sales and class fees?
- Do you get paid by the class, by the student or by the hour?
- Does the shop expect you to pay a fee for use of the classroom or a percentage of your class fees?
- Who handles advertising for the classes?
- How often are you expected to have classes or workshops?
- How much time will be allotted for each class?

A good working relationship needs a good understanding of the responsibilities of both parties.

Attracting Students to a Retail Shop

After both you and the shop owner or manager have a clear understanding of what to expect and have reached an agreement that is satisfactory to both of you, you are ready to advertise and promote your classes. There are several tried and true methods for attracting students.

An excellent way to begin is to set up a space to exhibit the class projects offered or have an open house where they are on display. Many shops use the open house idea at the beginning of each teaching term. The teachers display samples of their work and are on hand to answer questions and sometimes demonstrate their painting skills. In this type of advertising, you should be able to explain the medium used, the cost of supplies, what the class will include, the skill level needed and approximately how long each project will take to complete.

Be enthusiastic about the joys of painting and the fact anyone can learn to paint. I've taught for many years and honestly believe this to be true. The students' level of ability may vary, but anyone who really wants to paint can attain satisfying painting skills. Share this fact with anyone who shows an interest in learning to paint.

Many students have told me they have wanted to paint all of their lives but either didn't know where to begin or were afraid they couldn't do it and would be embarrassed. Decorative painting opens the door to people who want to learn because we approach painting with such a positive attitude. Teaching people to paint by demonstrating step-by-step techniques is far more successful than the old "Paint something and I'll come around and tell you what's wrong with it" approach. When you lead students through a variety of techniques, explaining everything from brush care to color theory, learning to paint is a time of fun as well as achievement. Share this information with prospective students, so they want to be a part of the decorative painting world.

If you are asked to do demonstrations, you can advertise your classes while you are doing the demonstration. Incorporate bits of information about your classes in your dialog as you explain the techniques you are using. Pass out flyers with class information on them. Display business cards and invite interested watchers to take one. Set up samples of your work and a poster that tells about your classes—how long they last, what projects will be taught, the number of students you will take. "Space limited to——" accomplishes two things: It lets students know that if they are

Barbara Buttram: The Dedicated Teacher

Occasionally, in the world of decorative painting you will find a teacher who is so enthusiastic about teaching that her only ambition is to share her knowledge and spread the word about what fun it is to be a painter. One such teacher is Barbara Buttram. Barbara doesn't publish books or packets, own a shop or even have an in-home studio. Barbara teaches! She does it virtually anywhere she can find students who want to learn.

If your town doesn't have a shop where you can hold classes, don't let that stop you. Barbara found or created teaching opportunities at community schools and through the park department. She has taught senior citizens (the class she refers to as "The Kids"), the physically limited and men, women and children. She was instrumental in obtaining a decorative painting booth at the state fair and setting up a special category for decorative painters in the art competition. Her enthusiasm has brought many people into the world of decorative painting.

Barbara now teaches four classes a week at a large art supply store, but she continues to teach "The Kids" and other special groups who might otherwise never experience the joy of painting. ☙

interested they should sign up immediately or they might not get in, and it lets them know they will get enough attention because you will only take a certain number of students.

Another method of advertising is to offer a free demonstration occasionally. Set up posters or ask the shop owner or manager to list the times they will be offered in their advertising. Good classes mean more business for the store. Set up in an area of the store where traffic is heaviest, such as near the checkout counter. Be friendly and talk to anyone who stops to watch.

If you sell your work, you are already advertising your work. Make it more effective by including on your tags or business cards that you also teach. Include a flyer about your classes in the bag with each purchase. Set up a poster advertising your classes in a prominent place where you sell your work. Compile a mailing list and send out occasional newsletters listing your class schedules and a brief description of the projects that will be offered.

Charitable events can also be good advertising. If you are asked to donate work to a school or other charitable organization, include a short biography that explains what you do. Be sure to donate a piece of your best work. Some painters only want to donate the "dogs" that don't sell elsewhere. Save those for your garage sale. Donating your best to a worthwhile cause is far more rewarding, both personally and professionally. It's a real ego trip to learn that a piece you would have sold for around $200 went for over $1,000 at a benefit auction. You will receive kudos from everyone for your generosity and artistic skills. You may be commissioned to paint or find a new student.

Many home builders and real estate agents use a parade of fully furnished model homes to promote new housing additions. Contact the builders or show sponsors and ask who is decorating the houses. Then contact the decorators and offer to add hand-painted decorations in return for advertising your classes. You may even get a few commission jobs.

Community Schools and Park Departments

Many large cities and even some smaller communities offer painting classes through the local school system, community college or park department. Make a few phone calls to find out if this opportunity is available in your area. If they offer classes, but not decorative painting, offer to start a painting class.

The fees for teaching in city- or county-sponsored programs can vary greatly. Some schools pay by the student, while others pay an hourly rate. They may limit the number of students you can have in each class. However you are paid, make sure it is worth your time. It's OK to start small, and some teachers are willing to work for very little money to establish themselves as teachers. But at some point you should take an honest look at the situation. If you have good teaching skills and experience, you should be earning more than minimum wage. Some groups want to collect the money and pay the teacher at the end of the session. Teachers who have tried this do not feel it is a satisfactory way of doing business. Sometimes there are delays in payment. Ask to be paid at the beginning of the session for the students who have enrolled.

Determine who is responsible for ordering and selling supplies. Some schools include the cost of supplies in the enrollment fee. If that's the case, be sure the cost will cover adequate supplies. Otherwise, you may find yourself buying supplies to supplement the students' needs, and if that happens often, you will be teaching for nothing.

If your town is too small or too saturated with teachers, take time to drive to small surrounding communities to look for teaching opportunities. If there is not a shop in the area, check with the board of education or park department. They may have classroom space available for your use. This type of teaching can be very lucrative because generally you will need to bring in and sell all supplies. It takes some organization, but many teachers find loyal students who are grateful for the opportunity to learn in their own community.

Other Teaching Opportunities

Some large businesses provide recreational activities for their employees. If there is such a business in your area, contact the personnel department and discuss the possibility of offering painting classes.

Contact the local television station or cable TV provider and offer to demonstrate decorative painting on one of their local interest shows. Even if you don't get paid, you can mention your classes.

Home extension groups are always looking for good programs. Call and offer to do a program on decorative painting with explanations and demonstrations of several techniques, or do a paint-along for a nominal fee to cover supplies. Be sure to have business cards or flyers to hand out.

Teaching on a National Level

Once you have teaching experience under your belt and have achieved a degree of success in filling classes, you may want to try your hand at teaching on a broader scale. The best way to begin is to submit your work for consideration as a teacher at a decorative painting convention. Small conventions, commonly referred to as miniconventions, are usually sponsored by a local chapter of the Society of Decorative Painters or group of chapters in a state-wide area. These are held in the same location each time. The national convention moves around the country and is held in a different location each year.

To teach at these conventions, you must submit photographs of your work to a selection committee. The work does not have to be original, but if it isn't your own design, you will need written permission from the designer allowing you to teach it. Contact the national society or the sponsoring chapter for an application. Teachers are chosen far in advance of the show, so plan ahead and request information early.

There are definite criteria to follow when teaching at conventions, so read all the literature they send you. Each show has different rules, so don't assume you know what they want. They usually include guidelines to help you estimate what to charge for supplies. When estimating the class cost, remember to include the cost of patterns, photos, instructions, shipping, base-coating and all of the other incidental costs besides the basic painting surface.

You will be required to teach a certain number of students. Classes vary from fifteen to thirty-five students. Classes that are not filled may be canceled by the sponsors of the convention. Once a specific minimum is met, you are expected to teach, even if the class is not completely full. Do not even apply to teach at a convention unless you are absolutely committed to attending. You don't have an option of canceling at the last minute to attend a family wedding or a class reunion.

Occasionally, teachers may be accepted to teach several classes and then have one of them canceled. If that happens, you are still required to teach the remaining class, which can change the expense/income picture greatly. Be prepared to bear the expense of attending the convention to teach just one class. Don't count on the profits from teaching several classes to totally pay the expenses incurred in attending the convention.

---

*F*ive times a year brush manufacturer Loew-Cornell publishes a great newsletter, *Teacher's Spectrum*, with excellent articles by many well-known decorative painters. The articles cover virtually every topic of interest to the decorative painter, from teaching classes to getting on the Internet. For information on how to receive the newsletter, contact:

Loew-Cornell
Attn.: Shirley Miller
563 Chestnut Ave., Teaneck, NJ 07666-2490
(201) 836-7070; fax: (201) 836-4878

Guideline Plan for Teaching

✳ Estimate the amount of time needed to finish each project, then move the class in a timely fashion to meet those guidelines. One popular rule of thumb is to allow at least three times as long to teach a project as it took you to paint the project. Obviously this is not a hard and fast equation, but it does give a time ratio from which to work. Beginning classes move at a slower pace because more explanation and individual attention are needed. Advanced classes should move much faster, and many students can keep up with the teacher stroke for stroke.

✳ Be on time. Start and end the class at the designated times, so students will learn quickly that if they are late you will begin without them. You have a responsibility to the entire class to give them the amount of class time they paid for, so do not waste class time waiting for the chosen few who arrive late.

✳ Be prepared. You should have instructions for surface preparation, a pattern and a list of supplies ready to hand out to students. If you supply pre-prepped surfaces, have surfaces carefully prepared and available on time.

✳ It is especially helpful to have the pattern, palette and any special instructions printed and ready to pass out. Unless you are furnishing palettes, you must allow some time for the students to prepare their palettes and painting supplies. After a reasonable amount of time, begin the class. If allowed to dawdle, students can waste valuable class time "settling in."

✳ Depending on the size of the class, it is helpful to have more than one teaching sample available so you can pass one around while the other remains in view of the entire class. Another option is to have photographs of the finished piece. If you supply photographs, be sure the photos are clear and the color is accurate. Bad photographs can cause more problems for the students than you can imagine.

✳ If you demonstrate on a large surface at the easel, have the surface prepared and the pattern on so you don't waste class time doing your "homework."

✳ Allow extra time to explain difficult or involved techniques. Also, try to incorporate explanations of blending techniques, color theory and stroke work in your instructions as you go along. All this information is important and needs to be repeated often. Every time you have a chance, whether it is helping an individual or demonstrating at the easel, go over the technique again.

TEACHER CONTRACT & PROJECT INFORMATION SHEET
SOCIETY OF DECORATIVE PAINTERS
27TH ANNUAL MEETING AND CONVENTION
WICHITA, KANSAS, MAY 1999 _____

OFFICE USE ONLY

Membership Number_____
Name (Please Print) Last_____First_____( )CDA ( )MDA
Address_____
City_____State_____Zip_____
Phone Number - Home(____)_____Business(____)_____
FAX(_____)_____E-Mail_____
Social Security or Taxpayer ID Number_____
Name as shown on Social Security Card_____
Team Teacher Name_____Membership Number_____( )CDA ( )MDA

*For a 4 or 6 hour class the total teaching fee is $60 per hour per class ($240 for a 4-hour class , $360 for a 6-hour class) for single or team-taught classes. Maximum enrollment for a 4-or 6-hour class is 30 students.
For Intensive Advanced Studies (IAS) the total teaching fee is $60 per hour per class ($480 for 8 hour, $720 for 12 hours) for single or team-taught. Maximum enrollment for **IAS is 20 students.

PROJECT TITLE: (40 characters or less)

□□□□□□□□□□□□□□□□□□□□

□□□□□□□□□□□□□□□□□□□□

PROJECT CATEGORY (check only one)
□Animals & Birds □Flowers □Folk Art □Fruits & Vegetables □Landscapes □People □Seasonal
□Still Life □Theory/Technique/Project □Theory/Technique/Worksheet □Traditional Stroke Art

This project is (check only one); □4 hour □6 hour □8 hour □12 hour

Split classes, held on two separate days will be conducted in the following manner: Four-hour classes will not be split. Six-hour classes will be split into 4 and 2 hours. Eight-hour classes will be split into 4 and 4 hours. Twelve-hour classes will be split into 6 and 6 hours. Are you requesting to teach a split class? □ Yes □ No

Are you willing to teach this class more than one time? □ Yes □ No
IAS classes can only be taught **1 (one)** time.

LEVEL OF DIFFICULTY (check only one):
□**Beginning Basic**:Student need little or no experience in the skills in the stated medium. (Classes are 4 or 6 hours.)
□**Beginner**:Student should have knowledge of the basic fundamentals and minimum skills in the stated medium. (Classes are 4 or 6 hours.)
□**Intemediate**:Student should have had previous classes, some experience and well-developed skills in the stated medium. (Classes are 4 or 6 hours.)
□**Advanced**:Student should have had extensive experience and highly developed skills in the stated medium. (Classes are 4 or 6 hours.)
□**Intensive Advanced Study**: Provides a challenging experience for advanced painters proficient in the stated medium. (Classes are 8 or 12 hours.)

It is not permissible to sell, publish or teach this project prior to the first day of Convention. It may be published for release at this Convention or between Convention and the following January, providing you check "yes" in the box below. This will be indicated in the *Convention Special*. If you check "no," you may not publish the project until January 1, 2000. □ Yes □ No

If you are requesting special scheduling; please state reason (i.e. booth set-up, tear-down, judging, etc.)
_____

Length & width of painting surface_____
Cost of project (See TAY, pg. 2-Considerations to determine supply fee)_____
Comments regarding project cost (i.e. frame not included, mat included, etc.)_____
Primary medium (acrylic, acrylic-gouache, fabric dye, oils, watercolor, etc.)_____
Type of painting surface (canvas, fabric, glass, masonite, wood, etc.)_____
Specific supplies requested: 1._____2._____3._____
4._____5._____6._____7._____

Goal, objective and bio if theory class or IAS class:_____
_____
_____
_____

Sample teacher's contract for the National Society of Decorative Painters.

SDP CONVENTION TEACHER POLICIES

1. All who teach at Convention must be members in good standing of the SDP for two years: 12 months prior to the submission deadline as well as 12 months during the convention year. Submissions will be refused if not postmarked on or before **June 16, 1998.**
2. Each teacher is limited to submitting three (3) projects.
3. Classes submitted for teaching purposes must be:
    A. Original projects.
    B. Project-oriented theory/technique classes must be originial. The technique may have been taught previously at an SDP national Convention or elsewhere.
    C. Worksheet- or notebook-oriented theory/technique classes may have been taught previously at national Convention or elsewhere. The accompanying photograph must be the same as previously submitted.
4. Teachers publishing or teaching a project must so indicate at the appropriate place on the Teacher Contract & Project Information Sheet, so it can be noted in the *Convention Special*. If not noted, publishing or teaching prior to the following January is prohibited.
5. Selling, publishing or teaching projects is prohibited prior to the first day of Convention.
6. Teachers may practice-teach the project once at the local level (i.e. chapter, local shop or regular teaching location).
7. The photograph, which must accompany the Teacher Contract & Project Information Sheet, must be a 5x7 color photo. ALL SUBMITTED PHOTOS BECOME PROPERTY OF THE SDP AND WILL NOT BE RETURNED.
8. Submitted photograph(s) must be free of signature or specific product names on the front. Do not write on the color photograph!
9. The project, as shown in the *Convention Special* photograph, must be provided to students at the specified cost. Any part not included must be indicated on the Teacher Contract & Project Information Sheet.
10. If specific supplies are required for the project, they must be noted on the Teacher Contract & Project Information Sheet.
11. A painted sample must be on display in the Class Sales Area. Sample may be removed when teaching class. Sample(s) must be delivered to Class Sales area by the specified time. Class sample(s) must be picked up from the Class Sales area at the designated time. Sample(s) will be disposed of at the local level 30 days after the close of Convention.
12. Sufficient supplies to complete the project must be provided for all students. (See To Assist You, pg. 2, Considerations, b. Paint.)
13. Class time must not be misused by selling, or advocating positions or points of view.
14. The "No Smoking" policy must be observed by both teachers and students.
15. A teacher may not cancel the obligation to teach once the project has been selected for Convention. Cancellations can only be considered in the event of personal or family emergencies. Otherwise, the teacher cannot be considered for teaching in subsequent Convention years. **However, due to insufficient enrollment, classes may be canceled by SDP (see To Assist You, pgs. 1-2, Cancellation of Classes).**
16. All first-time teachers are required to attend the Convention Teacher Orientation.
17. No Convention teacher may hold a seminar in the Convention city one week prior to Convention. (See To Assist You, pg. 4 Seminars Held in Convention City before or after Convention).
18. The use of aerosol sprays in conjunction with classes inside at any Convention facility is not permitted (Board Action 6/93)

COPYRIGHT

The NSTDP, as an association of artists, is committed to the protection of your original artistic and literary work and to minimizing the NSTDP's liability exposure. Please carefully read the following document. Your signature, which signifies that you have read and agree to this contract, is required for your participation in teaching at the Society's national Convention in Phoenix in 1998.
Ownership. I represent and warrant that I am the owner of the artwork covered by this agreement and that the artwork has been created by me and is original and not a copy, in whole or in part, of an existing work or design. I further represent and warrant that the artwork does not infringe any copyright, trade secret, trademark, service mark or other property right of any third individual.
Indemnity. I agree to indemnify and hold NSTDP officers, directors, employees, members, agents and assigns harmless from any and all costs, claims, damages, expenses, losses and demands of any type (including legal expenses) incurred by or against NSTDP as a result of or in connection with any claim made or alleged that the artwork infringes any copyright, trade secret, trademark, service mark and other property right of any third party, or as a result of a breach of the representation or warranty contained in the preceding paragraph.
NSTDP Rules. I agree that NSTDP may investigate any claim that I have violated the terms of this or any other agreement with NSTDP, including but not limited to claims of infringement (referred to as "Investigation"). Any Investigation shall be undertaken by NSTDP in the manner, scope and methods as decided by NSTDP in its sole discretion in accordance with NSTDP Bylaws. I agree to fully cooperate with any Investigation. NSTDP may take any action it deems necessary following such investigation, including but not limited to: termination of any pending or future offer to teach, publish or in any manner promote me or my artwork; disclosure of any such action to any third party, include but not limited to affiliates of NSTDP; any other action deemed appropriate in the sole discretion of NSTDP. NSTDP may act through its executive council or any designee or agent authorized by NSTDP to act for NSTDP in the Investigation.

I have read and understand all information offered in the Teacher Contract & Project Information Sheet including the Teacher Policies. I agree to comply with all policies and understand that failure to comply is grounds for disqualification and/or one year suspension.

_____   _____
Teacher Signature   Date

_____   _____
Team Teacher Signature   Date

_____   _____
Society of Decorative Painters Signature   Date

IF PROJECT IS ACCEPTED, A COPY OF THIS CONTRACT, SIGNED BY SDP, WILL BE RETURNED TO YOU.

RETURN THIS AGREEMENT WITH YOUR 5"X7" COLOR PHOTOGRAPH, RETURN RECEIPT REQUESTED, POSTMARKED ON OR BEFORE JUNE 16, 1998, TO:

Society of Decorative Painters, 393 N. McLean Blvd., Wichita, KS 67203-5968

REV 7/1997

1998 *Las Vegas* CREATIVE PAINTING CONVENTION

Phone: (702) 221-8234 • Fax: (702) 221-8527   Hours: 11 a.m. - 6 p.m., <u>PACIFIC</u> time

TEACHER INVITATION

The next annual Las Vegas Creative Painting Convention will be held at the Tropicana hotel/casino in fabulous Las Vegas, Feb. 22 - 27, 1998 (tentative dates), and you are invited to submit to teach. Please read all instructions carefully and completely before filling in the teacher application(s).

THE DEADLINE FOR PROJECT SUBMISSION IS FEBRUARY 15, 1997.
<u>Submissions must be RECEIVED (not just postmarked) by the deadline of Feb. 15, 1997.</u>

CATEGORIES: You may submit to teach in three categories: classes (limit 4), audit or lecture (limit 2), and demo (limit 1).

COLOR PHOTO: You will need to submit a standard size COLOR photo of the finished painting with each application. If a 4" x 6" photo is used, leave about 1/4" of background showing all around the edge so we can trim it to 3 1/2" x 5" without cutting off the painted project. Class selections are made by a committee of 4 teachers and the convention director, with their decisions based on merit, teachability, and expected student enthusiasm. The color photo is the most important factor in the class selection process. Avoid blurry images, and we suggest using contrasting solid backgrounds. Photos of projects not accepted may not be returned due to the extensive amount of time it would take for sorting and mailing.

too small: better:

CLASS LENGTH: Class scheduling will permit either 3, 4, or 6-hour class sessions. A majority of students should be able to complete the project within the allotted class time. Please plan your class time accordingly. Higher priority will be given to 3 or 4-hour classes than to 6-hour classes. We can only schedule two 6-hour sessions per day in a room, whereas we can schedule three 4-hour sessions per day in that same room, allowing us to serve 50% more students. This becomes more important with increasingly higher annual attendance, and a limited number of classrooms. Some 6-hour sessions will be selected, but the number is very limited. We will also select no more than three intensive study sessions, at 8 hours each.

TEACHER FEES: Teachers will be paid at the rate of $3 per hour per student. ($9 per student for a 3-hour class; $12 per student for a 4-hour class; and $18 per student for a 6-hour class). Payment will be for actual registered attendance. It is the teacher's responsibility to collect class admission tickets, and turn them in to Jay Sharp at the convention office. Payment for class fee and supply cost will be based fully on number of tickets turned in, and checks will be mailed within 72 hours after the close of the convention. Maximum class size will be 36 students, and 60 for audits.

SUPPLIES: At the beginning of class, the teacher should provide the following to each student: The painting surface, prepared and ready to be painted on, paint, printed instructions, a color photo of the finished project, and any other "unusual" supplies that the student would not normally have for a class. The supply charge listed on the application will be published in the class directory, and cannot be changed. Distribution of manufacturer's samples to students, including paint, is encouraged since it keeps the students' costs lower, and benefits the manufacturer by allowing the students to try-out new products.

NON-PUBLISHED REQUIREMENT: Every project submitted must be unpublished, and must remain unpublished until after being taught at the convention. This includes books, packets, videos, and magazine articles. The project may have been previously taught elsewhere, but remember the newer and more exclusive the project is, the more likely it is to fill multiple sessions at this convention. Publication *after* being taught, especially as a packet, *is* encouraged.

MONITORS: Monitors are not provided by the convention. Teachers should arrange for their own class monitors if desired. We can provide you with a contact who may be able to assist you in locating a volunteer, or you may enlist the aid of a student at the beginning of class.

REGISTRATION: Teachers need NOT register for the convention unless taking a class from another teacher. No membership is required in any organization, and no subscriptions to any publications are required.

CLASS CANCELLATION: Any class not "sold" to at least 10 students by the time 1,000 have registered may be cancelled.

MAILING INSTRUCTIONS: Make a copy of the application for each item submitted, and clip (do NOT staple, tape, or glue) the color photo of your design to the application. Send submissions by REGULAR MAIL to Creative Painting, P.O. Box 80720, Las Vegas, NV 89180. If you are sending by UPS, Federal Express, or any method which requires a signature, do NOT use the P.O. box. Send those submissions to Creative Painting, 2875 Santa Margarita St., Las Vegas, NV 89102. Notification of acceptance will be mailed within 60 days of the deadline.

continued on next page...

Sample teacher invitation for the Las Vegas Creative Painting Convention.

TEACHER INVITATION, page 2

OTHER TERMS AND POLICIES:
Teachers will have spill cleaning/stain removing substance in class at all times, will exercise care with all paint materials, and will hold harmless the Las Vegas Creative Painting Convention for any such damage which may result.

Teachers are also invited to exhibit at the convention. We will make every effort to arrange your schedule so you would not be teaching during the exhibit hours. No guarantee, but we'll try.

A teachers' meeting will be held at the beginning of the convention. Anyone teaching at the Creative Painting convention for the first time is REQUIRED to attend.

Critique cards are given to each student for each class. These will be forwarded to teachers after the convention.

It will be a pleasure to welcome you to Las Vegas in 1998 for the convention. I know you will be impressed with the planning and execution of this event, and all the fun "extras" that Las Vegas has to offer.

Remember, all project submissions must be received by Feb. 15, 1997. Should you have any questions, please call Jay Sharp at (702) 221-8234, 11:00 am - 6:00 pm PACIFIC time.

PACKET OPTION: Should you wish to release your design in packet form after it has been taught at the convention, please consider listing it for sale through Packet Warehouse. The deadline of November 30, 1996 is approaching for the 10th annual Packet Warehouse catalog, to be released at the 1997 Las Vegas Creative Painting convention. We're planning an expanded advertising campaign for 1997, and hope to at least double the volume of packets sold compared to the previous year.

To submit packets for the 1997 catalog we need:
- packet marketing agreement (for new artists, see coupon below to get a copy)
- 3 copies of the packet
- An extra photo from the packet with the following info written on the back:
    Title, Price, Size, Medium (acrylic or oil or watercolor, etc.) and
    skill level (optional to label as beginner, intermediate, or advanced)
- A fee of $5.00 per photo to cover the cost of making a halftone for printing in the catalog.

Please help make this the best edition of the catalog ever by including your packets. The deadline is November 30, 1996, but of course you may send them earlier than that. Sending packets now for publication in the catalog does NOT violate the requirement that your submission remain unpublished since the catalog is not released until the convention dates.

JAY RECOMMENDS READING BEFORE SUBMITTING:

"Photographing Your Artwork" is a wonderful new packet by Connie Parkinson. It contains excellent information on film type, lighting, background surface and framing. It covers the special problems of photographing your work that are unique to our industry. You'll find the information very helpful both for packet photos and for submitting to teach at conventions. It sells for $6.50, and I have them in stock here. I urge you to order a copy, and recommend it so highly that *I'll cover the shipping* (saving you $2.00). Just send $6.50 and request item #36500.

"How To Make A Packet" is also available with helpful hints on layout design, photography, writing, packaging, and more. I'll even cover the shipping for you on this too; Just send $3.50 and request item #10014.

- - - - - - - - - - - - - - - - - PUBLICATION ORDER FORM - - - - - - - - - - - - - - - -

Please send the following to me right away:

❑ "Photographing Your Artwork"
by Connie Parkinson
item #36500, price $6.50

❑ "How To Make A Packet"
item #10014, price $3.50

❑ Packet Warehouse marketing agreement
(no charge)

Name _____

Address _____

City _____ State _____ Zip _____

please include payment with order and mail to:
CREATIVE PAINTING
P.O. Box 80720, Las Vegas, NV 89180

If ordering both "Photographing Your Artwork" and "How To Make A Packet" you can call (702) 221-8234, from 11am - 6pm Pacific time, and charge it to Mastercard or Visa. Your order will be rushed right out in the next day's mail. Charge card orders may also be faxed anytime to 702-221-8527.

1998 *Las Vegas* CREATIVE PAINTING CONVENTION

Phone: (702) 221-8234 • Fax: (702) 221-8527   Hours: 11 a.m. - 6 p.m., <u>PACIFIC</u> time

OFFICIAL TEACHER APPLICATION   <u>DEADLINE: FEB. 15, 1997</u>

(Tentative 1998 convention dates: Sunday, Feb. 22nd - Friday, Feb. 27th)

CLIP (do NOT staple, tape, or glue) COLOR PHOTO OF DESIGN TO THIS APPLICATION
SEE IMPORTANT MAILING INFORMATION AT BOTTOM OF PAGE!

CLASSIFICATION

❑ Demo: (45 to 50 minutes each)
Will you teach this demo even if you are NOT selected to teach another class? (circle one):   YES   NO

Note: Demos are NOT paid for by Creative Painting, but often have an exhibiting sponsor, who assumes responsibility for payment of the teacher fee. Literature and/or sample merchandise may be distributed, but the emphasis should remain on education, not sales.

❑ Audit: ❑ 1 hour   ❑ 2 hours
Will you teach this audit even if you are NOT selected to teach another class? (circle one):   YES   NO

A charge for any supplies provided to the attendees is optional. (Complete the supply information below)

❑ Class: ❑ 3 hours   ❑ 4 hours   ❑ 6 hours
          ❑ 8 hour intensive study (two 4-hr. sessions)
(be sure to complete ALL class information below)

CLASS INFORMATION

Project Title:_____

Medium Used: ❑ Acrylics, brand: _____
             ❑ Fabric dyes, brand: _____
             ❑ Watercolor, brand:_____
             ❑ Oils, brand: _____
             ❑ Other:_____

Skill Level: ❑ Beginner (slow pace, teacher assistance)
            ❑ Intermediate (avg. pace, some assistance)
            ❑ Advanced (fast pace, little assistance)

Size of painting surface: _____

What is the surface? _____
     (give description, such as wood sled, stretched canvas, etc.)

Supplies furnished by teacher (other than paints):

_____
_____

Supplies to be brought by student:

_____
_____

Supply cost to student $_____
     (round cost up to nearest dollar. Price must be adhered to)

TEACHER INFORMATION

Name:_____

Address:_____

City_____ State ____ Zip _____

Area Code & Phone_____

Area Code & FAX _____

Social Security #_____

Do you have a preference for teaching times?
     (We cannot guarantee this, but we'll try our best)
     ❑ mornings   ❑ afternoons   ❑ evenings

Do you plan to also have an exhibit? ❑ yes ❑ no

Based on student demand, how many times are you willing to teach this class? (circle one): 2 3 4

If selected to teach, how many class directories could you help distribute to painters interested in attending the convention? (circle one): 25 50 75 100

TERMS AND CONDITIONS

Certification of originality: The teacher MUST warrant that the design to be taught is an original design, and does NOT infringe on the copyright of another. Teacher agrees to hold harmless the 1998 Las Vegas Creative Painting Convention for any claims and/or suits arising from said design being taught. The teacher further agrees to assume responsibility for defense costs arising from any such action.

Teacher agrees to teach the design submitted at the time and classroom assigned at the 1998 Las Vegas Creative Painting Convention. Lodging at the convention and transportation are the teacher's own responsibility. Teachers will be paid $3 per student per hour based on actual paid attendance. (A 3 hour class pays $9, a 4 hour class pays $12, and a 6 hour class pays $18 per student). Attendance limit is 36 for classes, 60 for audits.

I have read and understand all policies, procedures, and rules on the teacher invitation and teacher application, and agree to same.

Signed,_____,teacher

Date_____

accepted by _____
for the 1998 Las Vegas Creative Painting Convention

Please complete a copy of this form for each item submitted. Limit: 4 classes, 2 audits, and 1 demo
IMPORTANT: Projects accepted must remain unpublished until after the convention.

Send submissions by REGULAR MAIL to Creative Painting, P.O. Box 80720, Las Vegas, NV 89180. If sending by UPS, Federal Express, or any method which requires a signature, do NOT use the P.O. box. Send those submissions to Creative Painting, 2875 Santa Margarita St., Las Vegas, NV 89102.

Sample teacher's application for the Las Vegas Creative Painting Convention.

Expanding Your Horizons

With wider exposure, other opportunities may come your way. Many of the manufacturers in the painting industry need capable demonstrators to work at conventions and trade shows. Some also sponsor workshops and seminars, and they occasionally hire local painters to help with these. They look for skilled painters to fill these positions and conventions are a good place to network and learn what opportunities are available.

CHAPTER FIVE

Publishing

How to Break Into Print

As your painting skills increase, you may begin to create original designs. If they sell well, you might want to consider selling the patterns and instructions for designs as well as the finished artwork. This leads into the area of publishing, whether on a very small scale by producing a few pattern packets or a much larger venture of full-color books.

There can be many turns and forks in the road to publishing success, along with lots of potholes and detours. The very best advice for a beginner is "Never gamble with money you can't afford to lose." In other words, start small enough so that, if your first attempt at publishing is a total disaster, you won't starve or lose your home. I have known people to take out large loans to finance their first book with only a dream of being in print and making tons of money. This is usually a very bad idea. Build a solid foundation under every business structure.

A Safe and Sane Beginning

The most prudent way to break into the world of publishing is to find ways to test the market without a major financial risk. There are several methods for accomplishing this. One option is submitting your *original* designs to magazines or book publishers. Their acceptance or rejection of your work is a fair barometer of its appeal. Rejection does not always reflect on the quality of your work. It may be your work did not fit with the publication's current editorial content. Remember magazines are seasonal. You should submit seasonal pieces at least six months or more before the actual season. If you submit timely projects to several magazines or publishers and they all reject your work, this could mean you are not ready to publish in today's market.

If at all possible, try to determine why your work was not accepted.

This isn't always easy. Most editors and publishers are too busy to spend time on lengthy critiques of your work, but some will take the time to answer your questions. It can be difficult not to take criticism personally, but think of it as a grade on a test paper. One failed test doesn't mean you flunked the course. It just means you have to study harder for the next test.

How to Submit Artwork to Magazines

Before submitting your artwork for editorial consideration, become familiar with the magazine. You should submit projects appropriate for that publication. Magazines published primarily for decorative painters include projects that require a higher skill level than magazines for crafters. If the magazine is for painters and woodworkers, you should submit projects painted on wood, especially if the wood design is unique and not too difficult for a hobby woodcutter. Many craft-oriented magazines use painted projects, but the projects usually are very quick and easy to do. They do not require advanced painting skills. The painting surface usually is readily available at major craft stores, is a very simple wood cutout or has a mail-order source. Magazines are always on the lookout for new techniques, new products and projects that are useful as well as decorative.

To contact magazines or publishers for submission guidelines, look for the address in the front of the magazine. It is commonly located in a box that contains the names of the editors and includes subscription information. There will be an address for submitting editorial contributions or requesting writer's guidelines. Include a self-addressed stamped envelope for the reply. When you receive the guidelines, read them carefully. They will indicate whether you should submit original work, photos or slides; if your submissions will be returned; if you need to include return postage and any other requirements. The guidelines also will tell you how instructions should be formatted and whether patterns should be included. Follow the guidelines as closely as possible. Many publishers require the instructions and patterns as a way of gauging not only how clearly and completely they are written but also how much space will be needed to print them and the skill levels needed. Instructions should be typewritten and double-spaced. Make the instructions as complete as possible, organize them step-by-step in the order you would paint the project. Include a *complete* list of supplies needed.

The following magazines are publications whose primary focus is decorative painting. The addresses listed are for subscription information. For the guidelines on submitting projects to be considered for the magazine, request writer's guidelines from the address listed for editorial contributions in the front of the magazine. Be sure to include a self-addressed stamped envelope (SASE) for the reply.

The Artist's Journal
P.O. Box 9080, Eureka, CA 95501

The Decorative Artist's Workbook
P.O. Box 3285, Harlan, IA 51593-2465, (800) 888-6880

The Decorative Painter
(publication for members of Society of Decorative Painters)
393 N. McLean Blvd., Wichita, KS 67203, (316) 269-9300

Decorative Woodcrafts
1912 Grand Ave., Des Moines, IA, (800) 477-4271

Let's Paint
DecoArt, P.O. Box 360, Stanford, KY 40484, (606) 365-3193

Painting
2400 Devon, Suite 375, Des Plaines, IL 60018, (847) 635-5800

Paint Works
243 Newton-Sparta Rd., Newton, NJ 07860, (800) 877-5527

Quick & Easy Painting
243 Newton-Sparta Rd., Newton, NJ 07860, (800) 877-5527

Tole World
1041 Shary Circle, Concord, CA 94518-2407, (800) 676-5002

As a general rule, it is not a good idea to submit the same project to several magazines at the same time. If it is accepted by two of the magazines, you will be forced to explain to one of them that it is no longer available for publication. There is a groundswell taking place among designers for changes in this area. They feel multiple submissions would give them the chance to accept the best payment offer and would help eliminate the problem of seasonal pieces being returned too late for submission to another publication.

The following magazines' editorial content focuses on crafts, but they also include decorative painting projects. As a rule, the projects they feature are quick and easy designs or projects that use new techniques or products. The addresses listed are for subscription information. For information on submitting projects to be considered for the magazine, contact the editors to request writers' guidelines at the address listed for editorial contributions in the front of the magazine.

Craft Works
243 Newton-Sparta Rd., Newton, NJ 07860, (800) 877-5527

Crafting Traditions
P.O. Box 5286, Harlan, IA 51593, (800) 344-6913

Crafts Magazine
P.O. Box 56015, Boulder, CO 80322, (800) 727-2387

Crafts N Things
2400 Devon, Suite 375, Des Plaines, IL 60018, (847) 635-5800

Handcraft Illustrated
P.O. Box 7450, Red Oak, IA 51591-0450, (617) 232-1000

Inspirational Crafts
243 Newton-Sparta Rd., Newton, NJ 07860, (800) 877-5527

Wood Strokes/Weekend Woodcrafts
1041 Shary Circle, Concord, CA 94518-2407, (800) 676-5002

Working With Manufacturers

If you use products from certain manufacturers or distributors, ask about having your designs included in project sheets or booklets they supply to customers. If you don't receive payment in money, they may send you a supply of free product. Many manufacturers, including paint companies, have an incentive program for designers and artists. If you include their products *by name* in a magazine, packet or book, they pay a fee. It's their way of rewarding designers for advertising their product.

Diana Marcum: Dare to Dream

Diana Marcum is an exciting example of all the wonderful business opportunities that are open to a creative, talented decorative painter. Although her first love is painting, her designs are licensed in many markets, including gifts, fabrics, buttons, sewing, cross-stitch and stencils.

Diana started on her road to success by entering contests and selling at craft shows. She submitted work to every contest for decorative painters she could find. Eventually she won a contest, and her work was selling well at shows. This gave her the courage to try to market her designs in packet form. She laughs when she tells about exhibiting at her first national decorative painting convention. She took twelve different packets, packaged in sandwich bags because she didn't know any other way. That was all she had in her booth, but she sold out and exhibited at two more conventions that year. She acknowledges that without the help and encouragement of more experienced artists, like DeLane Lange and Brenda Childs, she could not have succeeded as well as she did.

Her first books were published by Viking, but she eventually began to self-publish. As her work became known, she was approached by people in other markets and asked to submit designs for licensing. She continues to self-publish one or two books each year, but she also has books published by other companies. The scope of her business expands each year. Diana is absolute proof that creativity and talent combined with decorative painting skills can lead as far as you want to go. ❧❧

Contests

Another option is to enter contests sponsored by magazines and manufacturers. Diana Marcum, who is definitely a success story among decorative painters, got her start in this way. She submitted her work to every contest she could find. After she won several contests, she realized her work had market appeal and decided to try her luck with packets. She applied for booth space at a national painting convention. She laughs about how little she knew. Her packets were packaged in ordinary sandwich bags because she had no idea where to buy any other bags. She was so ill prepared that she says people were surprised to see her back the next year. Now her designs are not only published in the decorative painting field, but also in rubber stamps, dolls, fabric, buttons and almost everywhere else you can imagine.

Pattern Packets

One of the reasons decorative painters go into publishing is a simple time-and-money equation. You can spend an entire day painting one piece that you plan to sell for $35 and that is all you will earn for that day. If, however, you use that piece as the basis for a pattern packet you sell at shows or through mail order, you can increase your per-hour earnings considerably.

Many painters who eventually publish books begin with pattern packets. They are an ideal way to start. Initial costs are low. The average packet costs about a dollar to put together and sells for $4 to $10 retail. This is an excellent way to test the market to determine how well your designs will be accepted. Even small ventures, however, require planning. Look at the packets on display at local stores. Notice how they are put together, what is included and how they are packaged. With today's technology, you can do most of the work yourself, because of the availability of lettering fonts, clip art, computers and copy machines. It's a great improvement from the first time we did packets. We had the headers professionally printed and ordered them in great numbers to lower the per-item cost.

If you decide to try your luck with packets, include well-written instructions, a good pattern and a sharp, colored photograph or print of the finished project. In other words, produce a quality product. There are few

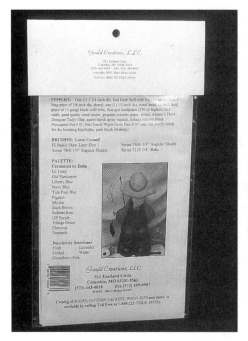

Mary Helen Gould

Mary Helen Gould self-publishes her own books and pattern packets of whimsical characters. She has a perfect organization to her pattern packets. On the front of each packet is a large, eye-catching color photo of the finished piece. The backside of the packet gives a list of supplies needed to paint the piece and a color photo of the back of the piece. Everything a painter would need to paint these adorable characters is on the front or back of the pattern packet. With this type of design, the viewer and potential buyer does not have to open up the package, which would ruin it for resale.

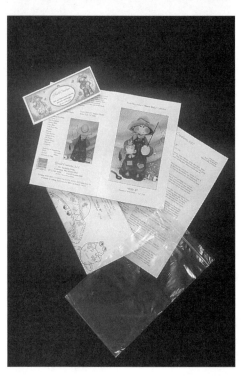

things more frustrating to a painter than investing in a packet with inadequate instructions, a poorly drawn pattern or a pattern that doesn't quite fit the recommended surface.

Some artists like to use a header on their packets, that is, an outside label that usually folds over the top of the bag and is stapled in place. It contains the artist's logo, name, address and phone number. Others use a heavy-weight paper that fits inside the bag. It has space for the photo and

There is one mail-order supplier who deals exclusively in pattern packets. For information contact:

Packet Warehouse
P.O. Box 80720, Las Vegas, NV 89180, (702) 221-8234

all necessary information. The photo is held in place with glue from a glue stick or with rubber cement. It looks professional and doesn't get wrinkled or torn like headers. The disadvantage to zip-closure bags is that they can be opened and closed easily, which allows thieves easy access to the contents. A stapled closure is a better deterrent to theft.

The picture of the finished piece should be clearly visible on the front of the packet. This is what attracts buyers. If the design is one with small detail work, consider including two photos, one shot of the entire piece and a close-up of the detail. It is an added expense that is worth the investment. No matter how cute or well done the design is, the packet will not sell if the photos are not clear and sharp.

Shop owners especially like a packet that has the size of the surface and a supply list visible without opening the packet. If the materials are arranged with this information showing on the back side of the packet, painters can buy all supplies needed. Also, it should clearly state what medium is used.

Marketing packets requires time and effort. Many distributors do not carry packets. Some mail-order catalogs handle packets, and the Internet offers another marketing opportunity. Sometimes it's a good idea to "bite the bullet" and get booth space at a trade show or convention. Watching the public's reactions to what you offer is a good barometer for determining if you are on the right track with your designs.

Copyrights

Copyrighting Your Own Work

When you produce original artwork, whether you sell the finished piece, packets and/or books, you should copyright your work. This gives you the exclusive right to determine how, when and where your designs may be used. The rights then belong to you during your lifetime plus fifty years.

Most people are surprised to learn that a copyright goes into effect as soon as a piece is created, not after it is published and/or registered. From the moment it goes onto paper it is yours, and no one else has the right to use it without your permission. It's a reassuring but scary thought. I've often thought ideas are like radio waves or television transmissions—they float around in the air until someone is in the right mode to receive them. Too often, I have seen virtually the same idea appear at almost the same time in separate parts of the country. If people are looking for something new, and if the country look is popular, it stands to reason the same general idea could occur to several people at any given moment.

It's common practice to copyright your work by simply putting a copyright notice on the piece that reads, "Copyright, 1997, Your Name" or by using your signature followed by the symbol © and the year. Sometimes the words "All Rights Reserved" are included, which extends protection to include all of the Western Hemisphere.

Legally, at this time, if you place a formal notice of copyright on anything you create, it is considered to be copyrighted, even if it is not registered. The catch is if you ever need to legally defend your copyright from infringement, it must be registered. Currently, legislation is being considered to abolish the requirement that a copyright must be registered if you choose to sue for infringement. This would make it easier for artists to protect their work. However, this will make it very difficult for you to make sure your designs are not violating someone else's copyright.

The decision to register a design or not is up to you. Consider the value of your work and whether you would be willing to take the time and expense of going to court to defend it. If you simply never have any intention of going to court if someone steals your idea, then it makes very little sense to register a copyright. Simply use a copyright notice on your work to remind people that it would be illegal to copy it.

Registering a Copyright

To obtain the required copyright forms and the current fee for registration, write to the United States Copyright Office, Library of Congress, Washington, DC 20559. Ask for information on how to register your original works or printed material and for any free publications that would help you. These forms will tell you the requirements to file your copyright. Currently,

---

Copyright Infringement Anecdote

*M*y favorite anecdote about the confusion concerning copyrights is one that happened to me. An early book of mine contained wooden cut-out Christmas ornaments that were a unique design, and they became quite popular. Members of the local chapter of SDP (Society of Decorative Painters) were taking part in a craft show held at a nearby mall. The first morning of the show I received several calls from friends, telling me about one member who was selling sets of the wood cutouts and including copies of the patterns. Being a peace-at-any-price personality, I tried to ignore the whole thing. Finally, after the president of the chapter called to say I should put a stop to it, I decided I had to confront the woman.

I went to the mall, walked up to her booth, picked up a set of the ornaments, removed the pattern and told her we had a problem because it was not legal for her to copy my patterns from the book to give away with the wood. Her reply was, "I didn't *copy* them from the book, I *traced* the patterns and copied my *tracings*." She acted completely surprised to learn it was only splitting hairs and was as illegal as photocopying directly from the book. It's a good example, however, of how copyrights can be misinterpreted.

One final note—I had good reason to doubt her sincerity. Either she was not quite truthful or she had very methodically traced the page numbers as well as the patterns.

---

the cost is $20, plus two copies of the work, such as two books or two packets. If it is a three-dimensional piece, accurate drawings or photographs are accepted. Books and packets require Form TX, while visual artwork such as fine art must be registered on Form VA.

Canadian and U.S. copyright laws vary slightly, so Canadian residents should contact their own Copyright Office.

Copyright Infringement

We should all strive to be original in our artwork, but how to define "original" is an area causing a great deal of confusion among artists. There is one question always asked when someone wants to learn about copyrights, and that is how much a design needs to be changed to make it yours. In other words, if a painting you see triggers an idea, how much of the idea can you use, and what constitutes changing it enough to make it original? As often as it is asked, you may receive a different answer each time. Several formulas are frequently quoted, such as "The design must be altered by at least 10 percent" or "Three major changes must be made." Neither is correct. My attorney says, in general, the governing rule is that if a copy is judged to take "the heart" of the design, it is considered infringement. It can be a subjective, individual decision in every case, but if there are substantial similarities, it is probably infringement.

Many people simply do not understand copyright laws and break them unknowingly. For example, I received a call from an artist who wanted information about creating and selling prints. He had painted several of the designs from my book, *Take a Gander*. His friends had raved about his work and told him he should have prints made to sell. He was obviously completely unaware of copyright infringement and was stunned to discover that he would be breaking the law.

There also seems to be quite a bit of confusion as to exactly what can be copyrighted. To put it in simple terms, an idea cannot be copyrighted, but the execution and expression of the idea can be. For example, consider painting strawberries on a wooden plate. A strawberry is a strawberry, and a wooden plate is a common painting surface, so the idea of strawberries on a wooden plate could not be copyrighted. If the design is used in a copyrighted book, does that mean no one else can use strawberries on a wooden plate? Of course not. However, the execution and expression of the design can be copyrighted, which means the exact placement of each berry and each leaf and the exact coloring can't be used. Also, if the strawberries fit a unique wood piece with an original shape designed by the artist, it would be covered by the copyright and could not be duplicated.

If you ever need to defend a copyright, consult an attorney who specializes in copyright law. A knowledgeable attorney can advise you of your legal rights and tell you what type of compensation would be appropriate.

Avoiding Copyright Infringement

There are a few simple rules to follow to avoid copyright infringement. Do not photocopy or reproduce any printed material. Assume it is copyrighted. Photographs, paintings or pictures from magazines should not be copied. When you buy a painting, wood piece, etc., the artist who created them still owns the image, you only own the finished artwork.

Photocopying patterns, books, etc., for teaching is another sticky question. Previously, one-time use was frequently allowed. As artists have

Examples of Wording for Copyright

The wording of a copyright is up to the individual author or publisher. The following examples will help you decide how to best convey your wishes in the matter.

Copyright 1998 Your Name
All rights reserved. Business or commercial use of these patterns or instructions is prohibited. No instructions, photographs or patterns contained in this publication may be reproduced (except for personal use) or duplicated mechanically without written permission from the publisher, except by a reviewer, who may quote brief excerpts. Individuals may paint these designs and sell them at bazaars and craft shows.

Copyright 1998 Your Name
All rights reserved. You may teach any and all of the projects in this book. You may also paint them for fun and profit. Photocopying and all other types of mechanical reproduction are prohibited.

Copyright 1998 Your Name
All rights reserved. Teachers may make one copy of a design per student for a class. A design may be mechanically enlarged or reduced for personal use. The designs may be hand-painted for fun and profit. Except for the exceptions above, no reproductions of any kind may be made from this book without written permission from the author.

become more aware of their rights, they have also become more careful of allowing anyone to photocopy their designs. Always read the copyright on the work to be sure. Unless it clearly states in the book or packet that it can be reproduced for teaching purposes, assume that you should obtain written permission. Many publishers feel having selections from their book taught in a classroom is good advertising, so they will grant permission for copies to be made for teaching purposes only. In your request, let the original artist or publisher know how many students you expect to have and when and where the class will be taught. You may call or write for permission, but ask for *written* permission. The answer can be faxed to you, but it should be signed by the author or publisher. Be sure to give the designer and source full credit, and do not sell the copies. They should be given free as class materials.

Using patterns from books and packets to produce hand-painted artwork to sell usually is allowed but only at the retail level. You cannot wholesale someone else's design without their permission. When in doubt, contact the owner of the design to ask if it can be reproduced for teaching or produced in quantity. You may or may not have to pay a fee or royalty.

Be sure to read the copyright on all patterns and books you plan to use. Some copyrights specifically forbid reproduction for profit, and the designs can be used for personal use only. Don't assume because you are in a remote location, no one will notice if you copy a design. I've had calls from as far away as Canada to tell me about someone giving photocopied patterns from my books with each of the wood pieces he was cutting.

Never copy licensed work such as Disney or Looney Tune characters. Generally, you won't get caught if you are selling at small local shows, but it is strictly illegal and should not be done. These multimillion dollar industries will not allow anyone to abuse their rights. Patterns from licensed designs almost always state they can be painted for personal use only, which means they cannot be sold for profit.

Videos cannot be copied. They also have copyright protection, and making an extra copy for a friend or student is in violation of the law.

Self-Publishing a Book

Publishing your own book is something a lot of artists did in years past, but today it is not easy or financially safe. It has always been a gamble, but today printing costs are higher, the market is softer and the life of a book is much shorter. If you feel you *must* self-publish, seek advice from someone who knows the market and can honestly evaluate your sales potential. Some people want to see their work in print so badly they actually refuse to use good judgment, even when it is offered by experts.

At one of the national painting conventions, I was on a panel to discuss book publishing. We discussed all the ways to publish, the expenses, the pitfalls and the possible benefits. All four panelists agreed and stated very clearly that with the rising cost of publishing, it is rarely a good idea for unknown artists to invest their life savings in publishing their own book. At the end of the program, one painter came up to us and stated that she had submitted her work to several publishers, but they had rejected it so she was going to publish a book herself. We all felt if several publishers had rejected it, it was definitely a very poor gamble to go full steam ahead and self-publish. But she was adamant. She thought her work was good, and she was going to publish it! In her zeal to have her work in print, she refused to listen.

To publish material rejected by professionals would be foolhardy at best, but this lady wanted so desperately to have her work in a book that she not only failed to see the dangers, but she also missed a great opportunity to grow. She should have asked why her designs were rejected and worked to increase her painting skills until she submitted work the publishers accepted.

Creativity and originality are essential to success in publishing. If floppy-eared bunnies are popular, another floppy-eared bunny will hardly sell a book. Unique touches must be added to make the design original. It is wise to include popular subject matter or color combinations. It makes the projects timely, but use them in such a way that your work stands apart from the rest.

If you think your designs are good enough for a book, your first course of action should be to submit your designs to a publisher who publishes books for a group of artists. In my opinion it is simply not wise for an untested author to self-publish. First of all, it is *very* expensive, anywhere from $15,000 to over $20,000 for ten thousand books, and you have to publish in that kind of quantity to bring the per-book cost to a reasonable amount for resale.

If a book sells for $9.95, an author does not receive that amount for each book. Books are sold to a distributor at deep discounts. The distributor then sells to the retailer at a lesser discount, who finally sells to the public for the retail amount. For example, the discount to a distributor may be given as 50-25 or 50-25-05. This means you deduct 50 percent from the retail price, then deduct another 25 percent from that number and possibly another 5 percent from the second number, so a $9.95 book actually yields only $3.73 or $3.54 for you. If your printing costs are $2.00 per book, you actually gross only $1.73 or $1.54. If your publishing costs $17,000 and the book retails for $9.95, you would have to sell well over four thousand books just to break even.

In today's market, with so many books being published, reorders from distributors are the exception rather than the rule. Chain stores don't need to restock titles because there is always a new book to replace the one that sold out. They also do not have the personnel to know the stock well enough to track and reorder fast-selling books.

Helan Barrick: Self-Publishing

*H*elan Barrick said when she enrolled in a painting class thirty-two years ago, the furthest thing from her mind was to someday begin teaching. Even more remote was the thought of publishing books with paintings and instructions.

She realized from the beginning that two things were important for teaching—to be well prepared to and to continue studying. Being well prepared meant that, for interesting and informative classes, she had to offer good, comprehensive worksheets, to demonstrate the lesson, to critique students' work and offer help when needed and to answer all questions regarding lessons and techniques.

Helan continued to study, experimenting in folk art, in painting figures, landscapes and still lifes, and in doing calligraphy, fabric painting and everything she could find to expand her knowledge and skills. She also tried different mediums—oils, acrylics and watercolors.

The time came when she wanted to share her knowledge and designs with painters who didn't have access to her classes. Publishing books seemed like a wonderful way to accomplish that goal. At the time, most decorative painting books were published by the artist who created the work, so Helan began producing self-published books. As the market changed, many artists found that higher printing costs and the large inventories and greater discounts demanded by distributors made self-publishing more difficult. They chose to let other companies or individuals handle their books. Although it has been difficult to compete, Helan continues to publish her own books, and as long as painters show their appreciation through their positive response, she will continue to self-publish. ❧❧

Publishing a book involves a *huge* amount of work. Consider the most basic elements of producing a book. First, you must create the designs. Whether you design new wood pieces or use existing surfaces, there is still a design process. Next, the pieces must be prepped and painted. The only job you escape for the time being is varnishing. Unvarnished work is easier to photograph, because there is no unwanted glare. Then, with all the fun behind you, you must begin the long process of drawing patterns, writing instructions, laying out the book, doing the photography, finding a printer and many more smaller tasks. It is a long road from concept to finished book. This is not a journey for the fainthearted.

Finding a printer can be a challenge. Many very good printers do not know what a painting instruction book is all about. One printer I used, who was not familiar with our market, asked questions like, "Can I reduce these black-and-white drawings (my patterns) so they fit the page better?" He didn't understand the patterns must be the same size as the painted sample. Some printers are not aware of how important exact color reproduction is to a painting instruction book. In the printing business, a good-looking color page is the only requirement. Matching a color exactly is not a major consideration. (Perhaps you have noticed a decorating magazine may mention the soft blue of the walls when the photo clearly shows green walls.) One more problem is that printers rarely know about the discount system in our industry, so they don't realize the importance of keeping costs as low as possible. They think if you are printing ten thousand books retailing for $9.95 each, you are looking at an income of almost $100,000, so why should you worry about a minor amount of $250? You should find a printer who is familiar with the decorative painting world or plan to spend some time educating one about your needs and expectations.

Photography is another very important aspect of producing a successful book. As with a printer, it helps to find a photographer who is familiar with decorative painting books.

Color separations are equally important. Without good color separations, even the best printers cannot produce a book with good color pages.

Two more expenses you must consider are advertising and warehousing. Remember that advertising is a major part of marketing your new book. It is very expensive and is one more deduction from the profit side of the ledger.

If you feel I am presenting a negative picture of self-publishing, it is because I want to make you completely aware of the risks. If you happen

Gretchen Cagle: Publishing for Other Artists

*I*n the world of decorative painters, Gretchen Cagle is rapidly becoming as well known as a publisher of high-quality decorative painting books as she is for her broad knowledge and excellent teaching techniques.

In 1982 Gretchen published her first book, *Heart to Heart ... Country Style*. Its success led to the publication of fourteen more books. As times changed, it became more difficult for a self-published artist and author to compete in the marketplace. Determined not to lower the quality of her books, she soon realized she would be forced to let someone else handle her publishing needs or to expand her own efforts to create more volume and a larger place in the market. She decided to increase the number of her publications by publishing the works of other artists as well as her own. Her business, Gretchen Cagle Publications, Inc., now represents and publishes books for thirty leading artists within the decorative painting industry.

Gretchen oversees every step of the production, does all of the copyediting and is the photographic stylist for each publication. Because she believes each book should represent nothing but the finest craftsmanship available in every area of production, her books are recognized as an industry leader in style, content, layout, graphics, photography and printing. Her desire for quality led her down one of the many paths to achieving a successful business with decorative painting as the foundation. ❧❧

to hit the market with something fresh and new reflecting current trends, you stand to make a nice profit.

Contacting Distributors

There are definite channels to go through to get your book to the end user. Distributors and wholesalers are a major link in this chain. You should send a copy of your book to every distributor of decorative painting books. Include the retail cost of the book and any minimum required, plus information on the discounts offered. The Society of Decorative Painters publishes a source book, available to members for approximately $10. It includes a list of distributors.

When contacting distributors, you may discover another problem of self-publishing. Distributors like to have a wide choice of titles from each source. If they can order a number of titles from one publisher, it helps with minimums and saves time and shipping costs. Some distributors don't feel it is worth their time to log the publisher of a single title into their computer system.

Independent Publishing

The problems and drawbacks to self-publishing has led several independent publishers into publishing books for other artists as well as their own. It gives them a larger inventory of titles, and they lower printing costs by printing several books at one time. Gretchen Cagle is one independent publisher who chose this route. She wanted to maintain the high quality of her books without raising the price. Virtually the only way to accomplish that was to publish a greater quantity of books.

Gretchen carefully chose artists whose work would fit well with the type of book she was publishing. Most, but not all, publishers have a similarity that runs through the books they publish. Some are known for quick and easy, trendy designs in inexpensive books that hit the market with a splash and soon disappear. Others opt for more timeless, classic designs, printing books that painters will keep and refer to for many years. When you consider submitting your work to a publisher, look for one who is publishing the work of artists with the same overall feeling you want to present.

Working With Publishing Companies

Finding a Publisher

Aspiring designers and painters sometimes worry about submitting their work to a publisher and having it "ripped off." Although this may happen sometimes, it has never happened to me. Reputable publishers realize they will not be in business long if they abuse copyright law. The creator of original designs and ideas is the fuel that keeps the machinery of their business humming.

There are a large number of publishers who handle the works of several different artists. Their books vary greatly in size, quality and content. Some publishers specialize in books sold primarily to the craft market. The books usually feature trendy, quick and easy projects that use readily available products. Chain stores like these books because they support product sales and appeal to a wide variety of customers. Other publishers produce books that support the products they manufacture, such as paint or wood.

Finally, there are publishers who choose authors because they feel their work is right for today's market. For example, Sue Scheewe publishes works from a wide variety of artists. Her authors paint in watercolor, oils and acrylics in styles as diverse as you can imagine, from primitive to fine art and everything between. The only common denominator seems to be the size and price of the books.

Gretchen Cagle Publications specializes in artists whose work would probably be classified as classic decorative painting. The artists' styles and mediums vary, but it is rarely quick and easy or trendy. That's why you should look for a publisher who markets books that appeal to you and that feature a style of painting similar to yours. If you paint in oils, creating involved projects with lots of detail, don't approach a publisher focusing on designers of quick and easy acrylic projects. Most publishers gear their books to appeal to a particular market.

The publisher's address and phone number are usually inside their books. Write or call to request submission information. Don't be discouraged if the first publisher doesn't jump at the chance of discovering a new talent. Publishers are very selective and may limit the number of books they produce at a given time. If they have an adequate number of artists, they may be publishing as many books as they feel they can adequately

Pat Olson: Letting Someone Else Do the Work

$\mathcal{P}$at Olson is one of the most popular authors of decorative painting books. Her designs are charming and timeless so her books have maintained a consistent place among the best-sellers.

Although Pat began to create designs for publication during the time when it was not only economically possible but very profitable to self-publish, she has always chosen to have her books published by someone else. Her reason-ing is that it takes a great deal of time, as well as a substantial investment of money, to oversee the process of pro-ducing a book. First, there's the job of finding a printer and photographer. Then, there are the layout, editing, photo shoots and all of the other details that must be handled just to bring a book to print. Finally, there are ware-housing, advertising, shipping, billing and stacks of other time-consuming jobs required to market the book.

In Pat's mind, it made better sense to let someone else handle all the work, leaving her free to create more designs for the next book or a series of packets. While she may net less money per book, she feels the time saved allows her to be far more productive, so the bottom dollar comes out the same. The fact that she has produced material for over sixty books and is now licensing her designs in other markets proves that her theory was right.

If publishing is your goal and the nitty-gritty details of business don't in-terest you, learn from Pat's example. There is almost always a choice of paths for reaching your goal, and Pat's choice certainly has worked well for her. ✎

handle. Other publishers are always in search of new talent. If your work is rejected, ask why and always *listen* to the answer. The criticism or advice you receive can be a great educational tool. Publishers want to produce a successful book as much as you do, and chances are they know the market better than you. Their advice can be very valuable. In understanding why your work was rejected, you may find out how to produce projects others will enjoy and buy.

You should also be open to having your designs included in a book with several other authors. Every step you take gets you closer to having your own book, so as you try to break into the market, be willing to explore every avenue. Each new experience is a stepping-stone on the path to success because you will gain insight and knowledge as you progress.

Publishers' Pay Scales

When a publisher produces your book, the amount you are paid can vary greatly. It is impossible to quote exact figures because there are so many variables in each contract. I must warn you not to fall into a trap of working for almost nothing. I once did part of a group book that actually *cost* me money. It began as a favor to a friend and to help promote a new product, two poor reasons for undertaking any business venture. Requirements changed as the book progressed. I had a very short deadline and had to buy all the materials at retail, paint them and ship them overnight express. I also had to supply duplicates of the products for the step-by-step instructions. The book did not sell well because the product used was not well known or readily available. In other words, it was a disaster. When the results were finally in, I lost $250 by working on that book, not to mention valuable time. It wasn't a crushing loss, but it was a very good lesson. Know what you are getting into before you agree to have your work published.

Most publishers pay a percentage or flat rate based on books actually sold. The pay scale can vary greatly. Well-known authors are in a better bargaining position. Predicting what you will earn is difficult because it is based on the number of books sold, which, in turn depends on popularity of content, circulation and other factors.

Some publishers pay a flat fee for each book title. That means that the author receives a specified amount, such as $1,000, for the designs in the entire book. This means you are selling the rights to those designs. If the book is popular and goes into reprint, you do not receive more money because you have released the ownership of the designs to the publisher. Some publishers pay a flat fee but pay extra if the book goes into reprint.

There is one other type of financial arrangement for authors that, to my knowledge, only one publisher uses currently. Eas'l Publications oversees the printing, then warehouses, ships and invoices the books for a specified fee. The artist pays the cost of printing and owns all rights to the book. The advantage is that printing costs are lower because Eas'l prints more books, doing several titles at each printing. By warehousing the books of a group of authors, they are able to offer the distributors a wider choice of titles, as discussed earlier in this chapter. The author realizes a profit of considerably more than if the outside publisher bears all of the costs and risks. One added advantage is the designs are evaluated by experienced publishers, who know the market and will not encourage the publication of a book unless they feel it will sell well.

If you are an unknown artist, you have explored your options and you find a publisher who wants to handle your work for even a small royalty, I recommend giving it a try. As a general rule, publishers want you to receive a satisfying return for your efforts. If a book sells well, but you do not feel adequately compensated for your time, you will not be eager to produce another book. It's better business when everyone is content. You will learn a great deal by working with an established publisher. If you don't earn great piles of money, you will have gained valuable knowledge. You can then use that knowledge to earn more money at a later date.

Videos

Videos are generally done by well-known teachers and authors who do a great deal of travel teaching. This is because videos usually are not sold in the same manner as books and are more difficult to get in the hands of customers. Most distributors do not carry videos, so it is up to the artist to get them to the public. Nationally known teachers sell videos at seminars and conventions and through advertising in major publications. In other words, the video sales are supported by everything else they do. Videos are similar to packets in that the artist must be willing to go out into the marketplace to sell them. However, the initial investment is much higher. They are not as expensive as books because they don't have to be done in

> To order videos, you must generally contact the artist. There is also a video market run on a subscription basis. For information contact the following company:
>
> **Perfect Palette™ Videos**
> P.O. Box 25286, Milwaukee, WI 53225, (800) 839-0306

large quantities. Once the initial video is made, you can order small numbers of tapes as they are needed.

Some individuals have achieved relative success with videos without being nationally known because their style or subject matter is unique and they are well known in a localized area. One Texas teacher who is particularly noted for the way she paints roses produced a video because of repeated requests. Her style of teaching would have been difficult to explain in a book, but the video allowed her to show paint consistency, special strokes and the other intricacies that make her style unique.

CHAPTER SIX

Working in the Field of Home Decor

Finding Opportunities

The idea of using decorative painting to enhance home interiors can be traced back to when people lived in caves. It has definitely evolved and changed over the years, but it has never lost its popularity. In fact, using painted motifs to enhance one's surroundings is one of today's hottest decorating trends. Faux finishes, stenciling and trompe l'oeil are so popular that many painters have ventured into the field of home decor as a well-paid outlet for their talents.

Paint stores offer classes and supplies for faux finishes. Everything from textured wall treatments to marbleizing is being taught in large building supply stores. Television shows feature people who are experts in the fields of stenciling, texturizing and glazing. If you have enough knowledge and skills in this area, your opportunities are vast. The market includes teaching, workshops and demonstrations; commissioned work from builders and decorators; restorations and designing. That covers a broad spectrum of earning possibilities.

If doing demonstrations or teaching classes appeals to you, locate suppliers of the products you use and ask about setting up classes or demos in their store. If they lack the space or simply are not interested in this type of promotion, ask if they would be willing to keep your name or business cards on file, in case anyone is looking for an artist with your skills. You may find do-it-yourself students or clients interested in custom work.

Call the program chairman of the local Society of Decorative Painters chapter, and offer to do a demonstration as the program at one of the monthly meetings. Most civic organizations are always in need of exciting programs. Offer to do a brief demonstration in exchange for passing out flyers advertising your classes or workshops. Home Extension groups occasionally offer members a day where instructors from the craft and hobby field do hands-on workshops. Community and vocational schools usually offer classes in home improvement techniques. Call the school and ask if you could bring a portfolio and talk to them about offering faux finish classes.

If you want to work in private homes or offices, there are lots of opportunities. First, contact local builders and decorators who hold open houses in their finished homes and offer to do small decorating jobs in return for letting you advertise in the homes. Most large cities hold a "Parade of Homes" to show new building and decorating ideas. Some are sponsored by builders and land developers and some by charitable groups as fundraisers. Either way, they can be an excellent advertising opportunity for artisans. My city has a "Decorator's Showcase" home each year. An older home in need of updating is chosen, and local decorators contribute their time and efforts to create a plethora of unique settings, using the most up-to-date ideas available. The house is open for preview before work begins and again, for an extended period of time, when the work is complete. The admission fees raise substantial sums of money for local civic organizations, which means a lot of people go through the selected home each year. Each of those people is a potential customer, so this type of promotion is often well worth the donation of your time.

Advertising Through Friends

If you have used your talents to decorate your own home, let your friends know you are interested in branching out and working for others. Friends sometimes hesitate to mention an artist's name if they are not aware you are looking for and eager to find new outlets for your talents.

Building a Portfolio

A written resume of what you have done is rarely sufficient in the world of art. Visual images convey your capabilities far more clearly and help potential clients see the possibilities. Always take good photos before and after each job, and use them to build a portfolio to show interested clients.

Andy Jones and Phillip Myer: The Business of Home Decorating

While Andy Jones and Phillip Myer are not typical painters who make a living in the area of home decor, they are certainly good examples of how far an artist can reach with his or her decorative painting talents. Both have impressive backgrounds in teaching and as authors of many painting instruction books. They have appeared on television and in videos and have had their work published in almost every magazine that includes articles on decorative painting or home decor. They have been active in both their local and the national Society of Decorative Painters.

Lately, they have focused their interests on interior design. Their combined talents have been used to decorate private homes and public works through-out many of the southern states. Always studying and expanding their knowledge and skills, they continue to develop new techniques, products and finishes to promote the art of home decor.

Phillip and Andy's philosophy of decorating would be an excellent guideline for all interior decorators to follow. They strive to fuse good design principles and wonderful painting techniques with clients' interests, hobbies and collections to create dynamic surroundings that clients are proud to call their own. They try to use their talents to weave together centuries of traditional art forms and finishes with the lifestyles of the '90s. Their decorated spaces are not only beautiful, but also function well as a background for the lives of their clients. ∽

Be ready to present a file of decorating ideas from magazines showing color combinations in the type of work you do. Include samples of textured, glazed and rag-rolled walls along with any other finish you do. An antique dealer once told me she arranged everything in her shop as it would be used in a home because only 5 percent of her customers could visualize the possibilities. The percentage may not be accurate, but her point is well taken. Decorators are usually up-to-date on what's popular and know how to communicate their needs. When you work with the general public, however, it's easier to explain techniques and finishes with visual images for reference.

Make your portfolio as professional as possible. Use a loose-leaf binder so you can add or delete pages as needed. You may want to decorate the binder with one of your specialty finishes. Oversized photos usually show the subject matter more clearly. Take both close-up and distance photos. For example, if your project is a piece of painted furniture, use a shot that shows the entire piece and another that shows the detail of the design. Do the same with room decor. Show a panoramic view of the room as well as a closer shot of the finish, stenciled motif or trompe l'oeil design.

Mount the reference material on an attractive background and enclose it in plastic sheet protectors. With the popularity of creating photo albums, the marketplace is full of choices for background papers and other materials to make the pages attractive. If you do calligraphy or are skilled at hand lettering, use your talent to write a brief description of each photo. If you have a computer, there are many clip art and font programs that would work beautifully. A professional portfolio will not only make a better impression on your client, it will also give you more self-confidence. You can let your work speak for you. One of the most frequently stated woes of professional artisans is although they know they are skilled and knowledgeable, they lack confidence when put in a sales role. Being able to show "documented" proof of your talents impresses prospective clients and bolsters your ego and self-confidence.

Setting Fees

When asked to quote a job, always give yourself time to estimate the job accurately by saying you will get back with a figure at a later date. You need time to evaluate the cost of materials and the time involved. What you charge should be based on the cost of supplies and the time involved in completing the project. It's a good idea to put your estimate in writing, so there will be no chance of misunderstanding.

Each job requires a special rate consideration. On some jobs it pays to quote by the hour, while others lend themselves better to a flat rate. If it's a renovation job, quote an hourly fee. This gives you enough leeway to cover unforeseen problems. Other options are adding contingency clauses or working on a retainer.

Basically, using contingency clauses just means if you do a specified job and don't run into unforeseen problems, your fee will be a certain amount. If problems you cannot predict or control arise, you will adjust what you charge to cover the extra time and work. For example, if you are contracted to do a faux finish on a wall that is wallpapered, the paper may look tight, but it may loosen and buckle in places when you apply paint. The paper then must be completely removed and the job redone. The contingency clause would allow you to charge for the extra work of removing the wallpaper.

If a client wants a difficult job done and you don't feel you can accurately estimate the time or materials, or if supplies are a major expense, ask to work on a retainer. The client agrees to pay you a set amount up front, which gives you working capital, and to pay the balance when the work is complete.

If you are a fast painter, charging by the job is usually better than charging by the hour because you will probably average a higher per-hour rate than if you charge hourly. Some jobs that can be done quickly and easily may look more difficult to the client or may only be quick and easy because of your advanced skill level. Those projects are better quoted by the job.

There is a certain art to making customers feel they are receiving good value for their money. When one local painter was hired by a decorator to add hand-painted artwork to a client's antique dining furniture, she estimated she could do the job in two days. The decorator explained that for what the owner was being charged, it would be much better to stretch it out over a longer period to justify the exorbitant fee. She then painted for short periods each day for several weeks. It is not a practice I recommend, but it presents a slightly humorous example of justifying the dollar/time ratio for a job requiring advanced skill but not a great deal of time.

Even small details like learning the terminology are important. There are always certain techniques and their related terminology popular with decorators, and knowing those terms adds to your credibility as a craftsperson. If you want to be known as an expert on applying faux finishes, learn the popular terms and be prepared to clearly explain the steps in achieving the finish. Believe it or not, you can charge more for doing exactly the same thing if you refer to it by an up-to-date, upscale name. As one artist says "The difference in 'antiquing' and 'glazing' is about fifty dollars an hour."

One other area open to decorative painters is restoration work. Repainting and restoring artwork in historic buildings is challenging. Although the demand for this type of work is not large, it is still a market to consider. Two local women have built a reputation as competent restoration contractors and are frequently hired to travel to other states to restore the artwork in churches. If you become an expert in a lost art, you may even receive free publicity. Editors are always on the lookout for human interest stories. The only major drawbacks to restoration work are you must be capable of physical labor and willing to spend time high above the ground on scaffolds to handle the demands of murals and ceiling frescos.

Painted Furniture

Individualizing New Furniture

If you love the idea of being involved in home decor but are not interested in using your talents to decorate entire rooms, painted furniture is very popular and presents the decorative painter with great opportunities. Virtually every decorating magazine and catalog includes some pieces of painted furniture. Both new and used furniture pieces are fair game for the magic brushstrokes that change an ugly duckling into a creation with charm and beauty.

To find a market for your talents, contact decorators in your area. Explain your abilities, and ask if they would be interested in your services. Shops that carry new furniture are sometimes open to the idea of adding painted designs to existing pieces to give their customers a selection of one-of-a-kind merchandise. If you decide to work with decorators or shops, be sure to make a portfolio of your work. Include photographs of finished pieces you have done, but also include photos of designs you have painted on other surfaces. This not only gives the client more choices, it also gives

Cynde Paveglio: Painted Furniture and "Found" Objects

Cynde Paveglio has found a wonderful market for her varied painting talents. She is one of those unique artists who can "do it all," and she does it very well.

To quote Cynde: "In the beginning I didn't make a whole lot of money at my art, but then I didn't know a whole lot about the trade either, like . . . pricing, market value, what shows to do, what shows *not* to do or where to market my skills. I did learn, . . . and soon I started to paint on objects other than canvas. I found myself attracted to making what other people considered junk into art."

Cynde combines a talent for decorating and floral arranging with her painting skills to create varied displays that attract a wide range of shoppers. She has gradually built a large customer base and limits herself to five carefully selected shows a year. Always creative, she looks for inexpensive, unusual surfaces to paint. She explains her "summer job" is to search for wonderful things to paint during the fall and winter months. She says her van automatically stops at any yard sale, estate sale, antique mall and flea market. She looks for anything unique, sometimes junk, sometimes treasure, but always something with character.

Cynde maintains a designer-size showroom in a craft mall where she creates cozy homelike room settings in her booth. She even decorates the large windows of the store and handles a variety of promotions to attract customers. Clients now bring their own furniture pieces to her for painting. The popularity of her painted furniture created a demand for classes. She now teaches several classes each week. This keeps her creating new designs, and she likes the feedback. Her students have some great ideas. ❧

them a better means of communicating what appeals to them and what they think would be suitable for their customer base.

The pay scale will vary from place to place and project to project. Since the surface will probably be supplied, your main concern will be the amount of time it takes to complete each project. If you have enough experience and skills to work in this manner, you should be able to estimate the time needed and charge accordingly. Remember that finished furniture can involve problems like slick surfaces and incompatibility of mediums, adding many hours of time spent on preparation and finishing. Take this into account when setting a price. Have a firm agreement, preferably in writing, stating your fee for each project. Payment should be made on delivery of the finished work.

If you work with a gift shop or furniture store that has delivery service, ask them to pick up and deliver the pieces you paint. This relieves you of any responsibility for goods damaged in transit.

Vintage Furniture

Decorators sometimes update existing furniture pieces with stenciled or painted designs. This market is handled like the home decor market. Look at the project, estimate the time and material it will take to complete the job and have a clear understanding about your fee, preferably in writing. Many beginners underprice their work, hoping it will help them break into the market. Don't fall into that trap. It's discouraging to work for nothing and bad business to keep changing and raising your price. Be realistic about what is involved in a job, and bid it accordingly.

If you like to haunt flea markets and tag sales, you may decide to paint whatever appeals to you and then try to sell it. One advantage is you can often buy interesting pieces of furniture for very little money. Once they are painted, the value increases greatly, giving you a larger profit for your time. A single chair can sometimes be found for about $5, but beautifully painted, a selling price of $100 or more would not be unreasonable.

Painted furniture sells well at upscale flea markets, craft shows and malls. Keep your designs and colors in tune with popular decorating trends. Arrange the pieces in a display similar to how they would be used in a home. Customers are not always creative enough to see the possibilities. By showing the furniture in attractive room settings, you can jump-start their imaginations.

Only you can put a value on your work, and the same equation applies to any painting piece. Add the cost of the surface and supplies, any selling expense and an hourly wage for the time spent. Of course, if the surface was purchased at a tag sale for a song, that changes the pricing equation. In that case, you almost have to price it by what I refer to as the "fair market value." In other words, charge whatever the traffic will bear. It helps to shop craft shows, malls and furniture stores and anywhere else painted furniture is sold to check out the competition. Use their prices as a guide to judge if yours are in line.

Expanding Your Inventory

To add to your appeal, don't hesitate to expand the inventory of what you can offer. A painter in Michigan who specializes in revamping vintage pieces of furniture, added wreaths and other florals to her booth because they complemented her painted pieces, were not time-consuming to produce and increased her sales. If your talents don't extend to floral designs, consider handling a few items on consignment if they enhance your merchandise and don't use up valuable display space.

If facing all the aspects of breaking into the field of home decor seems overwhelming, you might want to consider working with a partner. Sometimes two heads are indeed better than one. Frequently a business thrives faster if it offers more. For example, if your specialty is home decor, consider working with a seamstress who could handle draperies and pillows or a floral designer who could suggest finished touches to complete the decorating theme. The arrangement can operate more like a co-op than a partnership, with each party handling their own area of business but working together to increase the number of contacts and find new clients.

CHAPTER SEVEN

The Business of Decorative Painting

NOW THAT YOU ARE AWARE of all the ways to make money with your decorative painting skills, it's time to go back to the very beginning when your business was just a dream. We'll pretend it's the first day you want to start a business and you need to know what to do to make that business successful.

Throughout this book we have discussed ways to break into the decorative painting market and begin a profitable business. This chapter will cover the practices and skills important to every decorative painter who wants to succeed in business. Some information is essential and can mean success or failure in your business. Other subjects could be classified as "helpful hints"—the information isn't essential, but it may make the road to success a little smoother.

Networking

In recent years, one of the most popular terms in the world of business is "networking." If the topic being discussed is home-based businesses, the term grows in importance. An in-home business can be a very scary place to be. You are all alone, on your own, and occasionally you may feel confused and afraid. It helps if you talk to someone who has experience and understands how you feel. Through networking you learn from these experienced people. With luck, you may even find a mentor—a person who climbed the ladder of success and is willing to reach back and offer a hand to someone who is just beginning the climb. My personal experience is that decorative painters are eager to share and willing to become mentors. Many of the most well-known, successful artists are the most generous.

I remember one very special time, many years ago, when I was part of a decorative painting group called the Oil Rig. We were publishing our first full-color book. When the photos of our cover arrived, they were a huge disappointment. They looked more like candid shots of a garage sale than an appealing display of wonderful painting projects. For reasons that remain a mystery, I was the one sent to Amarillo to oversee a new photo shoot for the cover. During the shoot, we had a minor accident and the canvas of a painting was torn. Mary Jo Leisure was the only painter in Amarillo I knew who might have the supplies needed to repair the canvas. So, even though I was a complete stranger to her, I called to ask for her help. She was not only willing to help, she spent the entire day gathering the supplies to repair the canvas and even helped with the camera shoot. Her advice was invaluable. She shared her knowledge willingly. What a good lesson in generosity she taught me that day! Helping other painters along the path to success encourages the growth of decorative painting. Nurturing new talent and creativity expands the industry and keeps it from becoming stagnant. The continued growth of decorative painting depends on this willingness to share.

The Society of Decorative Painters

In almost every area of the arts, there are guilds and organizations whose main focus is to stimulate interest in the field and educate its members. Several organizations offer wonderful opportunities to network with other decorative artists. No matter which area of the business you choose—selling, teaching, publishing or home decor—I recommend joining the Society of Decorative Painters (SDP). The society is made up of local chapters in every state and many foreign countries. The individual chapters offer the opportunity to meet other artists and grow in the knowledge of the decorative arts. Contact the national headquarters for information on locating and joining the chapter nearest you. Membership in the national society is required if you wish to become a member of a local chapter.

With your membership in the society you will receive their magazine, *The Decorative Painter*. Each issue is filled with painting projects, including patterns and instructions, and informative articles about teaching, publishing and other subjects of interest to decorative painters.

Karen LaStracco: Gallery/Studio/Classroom

Karen LaStracco had a driving desire to paint and soon discovered seminars conducted by decorative painters. Before long she wanted to share her enthusiasm and knowledge by conducting classes. The town where she lives did not have a shop where she could hold classes, so she decided to open a studio in the downtown area. Because she does most of her work on canvas, a gallery-type studio rather than a tole shop seemed like a logical choice for displaying her art and teaching classes.

Pine Wind Studio Gallery is located on the square in Nacogdoches, Texas, population 38,000. Most employment is with the local state university, the timber industry and dairy and chicken farms. This makes buyers limited and retailers are very competitive. Karen said that several strategies help her reach potential buyers and keep them interested.

• She has a teaching studio at the rear of her art gallery and teaches five classes a week. She has been at the same location for thirteen years, so people know where to find her.

• She keeps regular gallery hours.

• Attractive presentations of artwork with frequent changes keep everything looking new and different.

• She has special art openings and shows, presenting themes of her art or a guest artist. She sends invitations and serves refreshments.

• She works with six other art galleries and shops located downtown to produce an annual "Art Walk." Over two thousand invitations go out to local and surrounding towns. This event is for families and provides a fun evening for them to walk downtown, view new artwork and see the artists at work. The producers receive free TV and radio coverage and other advertising. Their only paid advertising is newspaper space.

• She does programs for different organizations, including garden clubs, newcomers' clubs and service clubs. This keeps her work visible to different areas and is excellent advertising.

• Membership in several civic clubs and the chamber of commerce helps her network.

• She does demonstrations for art leagues and school programs.

• Each year she participates in two out-of-town craft shows to sell her art and painted wearables. This helps generate more mail orders.

• She always suggests that local clients who buy high-priced items "try before they buy." She delivers paintings to their homes, taking several extra pieces, and usually ends up selling more than the original order. Karen said, "I believe that happy customers are repeat customers—and I usually get referrals also." ❧❧

Conventions

The national society sponsors an annual convention that includes a large trade show, panel discussions, lectures and classes. The show is like a wonderland to anyone interested in decorative painting. Exhibitors include manufacturers, distributors, publishers and authors, woodcutters and suppliers of all types of merchandise related to decorative painting. Class projects are selected by a jury and many classes are taught by nationally known teachers. It is an excellent opportunity to learn new techniques and increase your skills.

There are also miniconventions sponsored by local chapters of the society. These shows also have classes and a trade show, but they are usually smaller than the national convention. Because they are not as large and are always held in the same location, the costs of attending are often lower. If you have never attended a trade show or large gift market, I recommend starting with a miniconvention. It will help you get your "sea legs" so you won't be completely overwhelmed by the larger national show. However, to completely understand the scope and importance of the business of decorative painting you will want to attend a national convention.

There are also privately sponsored conventions that focus on decorative painting. Any of these shows gives you a chance to network with other

The following five conventions are sponsored by SDP chapters:

Capitolers
Janet Snell
1273 Pembroke Court, Schenectady, NY 12309

Heart of Ohio Mini-Convention
Heart of Ohio Tole, Inc.
P.O. Box 626, Reynoldsburg, OH 43068-0626, (614) 452-4541

Mountain Magic
White Mountain Decorative Painters Guild
P.O. Box 681, Merrimack, NH 03054

Raindrop Chapter/Northwest Tolers
Cindy Lewton
3360 172nd Ave. NE, Redmond, WA 98052-5710, (206) 861-9103

Tole Country
Central Society of Tole and Decorative Painters
Vonna Garrett
3421 NW 68th, Oklahoma City, OK 73116

The following conventions are privately sponsored:

Creative Painting Convention
P.O. Box 80720, Las Vegas, NV 89180
Contact Jay Sharp
(702) 221-8234

Extrav—The Painting Exposition
(two shows annually)
2400 Devon, Suite 375, Des Plaines, IL 60018-4618, (800) 272-3871

Kaswood Expositions, Inc.
(two Canadian shows annually)
P.O. Box 172, Beaconsfield, PQ Canada, H9W 5T7, (514) 697-3436

Western Regional Decorative Painting Conference
Decorative Painting Conference
Conference & Institute Division
Dept. DP98, Utah State University, Logan, UT 84322-5005
(801) 797-0636

(Note: The contact people usually change annually, but most conventions maintain the same address for better continuity.)

artists, expand and develop your painting skills and broaden your business horizons.

Society of Craft Designers

There are several other organizations closely related to the decorative painting field that were also established to encourage and educate artisans. If your interest lies in creating original designs for manufacturers and publishers, I recommend joining the Society of Craft Designers. The society sponsors a conference each year in June or July. Its purpose is to afford designers the opportunity to network with other designers. The conference includes panel discussions and speakers who cover a wide variety of topics of interest to a business-minded designer. There are classes to familiarize designers with new products and techniques. Attendees have the opportunity to show their designing skills to manufacturers and publishers. The society is not for hobbyists who hope to be in business. It is for professional designers who create *original* work and want to grow in their knowledge and skills within the industry.

Society members receive a bimonthly newsletter that contains articles with useful information about the opportunities, as well as the problems, confronting professional crafters. If you are skilled at your art, creative and interested in designing projects for magazines, working with manufacturers or demonstrating at trade shows, the Society of Craft Designers will help you expand your scope and develop the business skills needed to achieve success.

Stencil Artisans League, Inc.

If the primary focus of your business is working in the area of home decor, using stenciling and related decorative painting, you should consider joining the Stencil Artisans League, Inc. The league is growing very rapidly and has almost forty local chapters across the country. Membership "provides opportunities for artistic and professional growth through education, certification, public awareness and networking." The league sponsors an annual convention with exhibitors and classes where you have the opportunity to learn about faux finishes, trompe l'oeil and the latest stenciling techniques. The show is held in late July or early August, and the location changes each year. Membership includes a quarterly magazine.

The International Faux Finishers Association

This group is dedicated to the promotion of the age-old techniques of faux finishes. It sponsors an annual convention with education and business programs. Beginners as well as professionals are invited to join. The organization is growing and wants to develop and expand its certification program, annual convention and educational and business programs.

American Craft Council

The benefits of belonging to this organization are access to group rates on health and property/casualty insurance, merchant credit card programs, discounts on shipping, rentals, magazines and much more. Members receive a bimonthly newsletter.

American Professional Crafters Guild

Sponsored by Sampler Publications, this organization offers professional crafters a bimonthly publication, wholesale buying program, health/life and property/casualty insurance, credit card processing and discounts on books and magazines. In addition to sponsoring the professional crafters organization, Sampler publishes *Country Business* magazine, which offers valuable information for professional crafters and in-home businesses. Although it covers the craft business on a very broad scale, much of the information would be very useful to decorative painters who are trying to build a profitable business.

Keeping up With the Times

Trade Shows and Conventions

When a great deal of your business success depends on staying current with changes in styles and colors, it is absolutely essential to remain up to date on popular trends. As frequently as possible, attend shows, scan decorating and craft magazines and visit home furnishing stores to see what's new. Watch for shifts in color trends and decorating styles. Be on the lookout for popular themes, such as birdhouses, garden and floral, painted furniture—

The following organizations offer information and sponsor annual conventions or conferences that would be of benefit to anyone interested in decorative painting and related fields. Write or call for membership information.

American Craft Council, Membership Dept.
P.O. Box 3000, Denille, NJ 07834

(or for more information)
American Craft Council/American Craft Association
21 South Eltings Corner Road, Highland, NY 12528
(800) 562-1973 (ACC), (800) 724-0859 (ACA)

American Professional Crafters Guild
P.O. Box 1397, St. Charles, IL 60174, (630) 377-8000, ext. 357

IFFA (International Faux Finishers Association)
Pam MacConnell, Executive Director
P.O. Box 837, DeBary, FL 32713-0837, (407) 668-9121
Fax: (407) 668-9121

Society of Craft Designers (SCD)
Marrijane Jones
P.O. Box 2188, 1100-H Brandywine Blvd., Zanesville, OH 43702-2188
(614) 452-4541; Fax: (614) 452-2552

Society of Decorative Painters (SDP)
Doris J. Hawkey
393 N. McLean Blvd., Wichita, KS 67203
(316) 269-9300; Fax: (316) 269-9191

Stencil Artisans League, Inc. (SALI)
Melanie Royals
386 East H Street, Suite 209-188, Chula Vista, CA 91910
(619) 477-3559; Fax: (619) 477-3559

For subscription information on *Country Business* magazine, contact:

Sampler Publications
707 Kautz Road, St. Charles, IL 60174
(630) 377-8000; http://www.sampler.com

There are two organizations that sponsor large trade shows featuring manufacturers and distributors of art and craft related materials. For show and membership information, contact the organizations listed below:

Association of Crafts and Creative Industries
1100-H Brandywine Blvd., P.O. Box 2188, Zanesville, OH 43702-2188
(614) 452-4541; Fax: (614) 452-2552
http://www.creative-industries.com/acci

Hobby Industry Association
319 East 54th Street, P.O. Box 348, Elmwood Park, NJ 07047
(201) 794-1133; Fax: (201) 797-0657; E-mail: hia@ix.netcom.com

anything that shows up repeatedly. Know which types of painting books are selling. If you paint to sell or teach classes, you should know which "look" is popular. Even if your work is classic rather than trendy, your market will be affected by these elements. Keep updating your material, dropping pieces or colors that are dated and adding new things to take their place.

Two shows I recommend to anyone who is serious about a craft-related business such as decorative painting are the annual shows sponsored by the Hobby Industry Association (HIA) and the Association of Crafts and Creative Industries, Inc. (ACCI). These shows are not open to the general public, and both have criteria that must be met in order to attend. Originally they were only open to members of the trade, such as wholesalers and retailers. However, they have recently opened a new category for designers. Now, with the necessary credentials and membership in the association and/or payment of the admission fee, designers can attend these shows without having a retail business. The HIA show is held in January and currently alternates locations among Dallas, Las Vegas and Anaheim. The ACCI show is always in Chicago in June or July. Call or write for membership and trade show information.

Gift Markets

Large wholesale gift markets are great places to spot trends and to pick up new ideas for painting surfaces. Gift markets are held several times a year in many larger cities around the country. The markets are only open to wholesalers and retailers, so you must apply for admission and meet certain requirements to gain admission.

A Notebook of Ideas

I strongly recommend having good reference material at your fingertips. As you plan the direction of your business, it helps if you keep a notebook of *everything* in the field of decorative painting that appeals to you. A loose-leaf binder is best because you can add or remove pages as your taste changes. If your main source of income is selling at shows, save every kind of resource material that applies—from new projects you want to paint to unique ways of decorating a booth. If you are a teacher, compile ideas for classes, new techniques or products to share with your students, even pictures of studios and ways to set up classrooms. Artists whose specialty is home decor should save ideas for painted finishes and color combinations, new looks in decorating trends, wallpaper samples and paint color chips. The notebook will become not only a file of good reference material, but also a source of inspiration.

Creating a Business Plan

Many businesses achieve rapid success because of a good business plan. Some people have a business plan and don't even realize it. They just naturally take an idea and map out the direction it will take. They are actually formulating a business plan without realizing it. They schedule their time well, set goals and implement actions to reach those goals. One creative seamstress I know took part in a major local craft show every year. Each year she set a higher goal than the year before, and each year she reached it. She aimed at a certain monetary figure she would produce and scheduled her projects and time to meet her goal. Some years this meant adding a number of smaller items that she could produce in short periods of time. Other years she added one-of-a-kind high-dollar pieces. She created mailing lists from the checks she received and notified previous customers of the upcoming sale. She kept accurate records so she knew which items were hot sellers. In other words, she had a plan. She planned to increase sales by a definite amount each year. She studied her history to let her customers know she remembered them and appreciated their business. Everything she did was to increase her business. Later, she went into selling gift items through home parties and achieved the same kind of success. Although she had no specific business management education, she knew instinctively that success depended on good planning, successful marketing, efficient use of her time and accurate record keeping.

If creating and following a good business plan doesn't come naturally, attend classes at a community or vocational school. Universities often offer seminars on starting your own business. Seek out small business groups offering educational opportunities. In some communities groups of retirees donate their time and expertise to advise developing businesses. A wealth of information is available. Take advantage of it.

Managing Your Time

The Pocket Calendar

Even if you haven't decided what side of the decorative painting business you want to pursue, you should start carrying a pocket calendar with you at all times. It should be small enough to fit in your handbag or pocket but large enough to hold notations on each day. It is especially nice if it has extra pages for notes and memos. Record all appointments, meetings and, especially, deadlines. This will keep you from overloading your schedule and making commitments you can't keep. As a friend once commented when I lamented taking on one job too many, "Of course you agreed to do it. You'd agree to your own execution if it was six weeks away." There's an element of truth in that for many people. Unfortunately, we all tend to overestimate our ability to do large jobs with a future deadline. We forget everything we've scheduled between now and that future date. Having the calendar handy puts it in black and white and helps you concentrate on the goals at hand. Another advantage of using a pocket calendar is if you decide to take a tax deduction for your automobile mileage, you can use it to record all business miles.

Using a Computer

If I could tell you one major investment to make for your business, it would be to buy a computer. Even if you only use it for bookkeeping and as a glorified typewriter, I feel it saves enough time to justify the cost. Due to the marvelous changes brought about by modern technology, computers are easier to use and startup costs are lower and far more affordable.

Consider for a moment, just a few of the things you can do, and do more efficiently, on a computer:

- Record keeping
- Accounting
- Profit and loss statements
- Letterheads
- Correspondence
- Invoices
- Instruction sheets for packets and books
- Supply lists and instructions for classes
- Mailing lists

As your business grows, you will find you can do more and more on a computer.

If you are computer illiterate, don't let that stop you. Remember, you don't need to know how a car is built in order to drive it. It is the same with a computer. You can easily learn to "drive" a computer without knowing how to overhaul it. Many computer stores offer classes with each unit they sell. Community schools offer excellent courses on the basics of using a PC. If all else fails, ask your teenager to teach you.

Outside Help

Do You Need an Accountant?

As stated earlier, if you want to build a business based on your decorative painting skills, you must change your mind-set from hobby to business. The sooner you accomplish this, the less time you will waste making poor business decisions. Gretchen Cagle's first words of advice for anyone wanting to be in business are to contact a CPA, listen to what he says and *follow his advice*. She has seen too many painters get into trouble because they did not understand the basics of accounting and taxes.

You may feel if you had bookkeeping in high school you don't need professional advice. That may be true, but what if your business grows?

Gail Bremer: Successful Tole and Decorative Painting Shop

$\mathcal{E}$ntering Gail Bremer's shop, located in a Milwaukee suburb, is like going to tole painter's heaven. It has such a wonderful selection of books, packets, painted samples and supplies that it's hard to imagine what decorative painting supplies she *doesn't* carry.

Gail's Brush and Palette opened in June, 1984, in a tiny 1,000-square-foot storefront. Gail had been teaching at a YMCA and ordering all supplies for classes. The need for space grew, and she opened a shop. After five years, she either had to cut back on classes and merchandise or expand. She moved to a 2,000-square-foot space in a more convenient location.

For many years, Gail did almost all of the teaching, offering five to seven classes a week. She now has local teachers handling eight to thirteen classes each week and sponsors twelve to fifteen visiting seminar teachers each year. The focus of the shop is still on decorative painting with classes available for all painting levels, from beginning to advanced. Classes are offered in oils, acrylics, watercolor and fabric painting. She has just started offering an evening woodcarving class.

If you ever have the opportunity to visit Gail's shop, take note of the official greeter, a Lhasa apso named Tillie. She knows all the customers and remembers those who bring her treats with an especially enthusiastic greeting. ❧

Before that happens, an accountant can be a valuable part of building a healthy, solid business foundation. He can set up the best type of bookkeeping system for your business. He can spot potential problems and help you avoid them. He will explain record keeping, financial statements, balance sheets, estimated taxes and many other facets of business you may overlook or fail to understand completely.

Accountants are familiar with tax laws, which change constantly, so they can advise you as to which business expenses are currently allowed and which are not. They know about money-saving techniques such as income averaging and about deductions a novice might overlook.

There are also certain areas where you should have expert tax advice. For example, many small businesses "hire" family members as a way of giving the family member money, and the owner receives a deduction from the IRS. To do this, the family member must actually work in the business and do meaningful jobs. You should know how to document their hours and the work they do, but you also must know about the tax systems involved.

When you hire employees, even family members, you become an employer and certain forms must be used. You are required to have an Employer's Identification Number, which can be obtained by filing IRS Form SS-4. An accountant can explain everything in detail and help you avoid costly mistakes.

If you feel you cannot afford the expense of a CPA, at least consult an accountant in the early stages of your business. You do not need to retain one on a monthly basis, but at startup it is a good idea. Think about the cost of mistakes you could make without sound advice. A good accountant will save you money.

Setting up an efficient system for keeping records also will save time. If you have to scramble at the end of the year, sorting through drawers and pockets for receipts, chances are you will miss allowable deductions. At the start of your business, knowing what is important information and how to record it can save hours of time and a great deal of money. Remember, even when a business is a hobby, the minute there is any profit, Uncle Sam wants his share. If he doesn't get it on time, he adds a big penalty. If you are ever audited, well-kept books, with receipts and invoices to back them up, will tell the IRS you are professional about your business and have good intentions. It also will help you defend any questionable deductions.

Hobby vs. Business

If you do not fall within certain guidelines, your income may be classified as "hobby" rather than "business." Losses from a hobby are not deductible. A hobby is an activity from which you do not expect to make a profit. The IRS says you are a business if you:

- sincerely try to make a profit
- make regular business transactions
- have made a profit at least three years out of five.

Some people think hobby income does not need to be reported. If you make a profit from your hobby, you must report your receipts, and you may list all the expenses you incurred to earn this income. If you end up with a loss, you are not entitled to a deduction in the amount lost, but you will not pay tax on the income.

Business Deductions

At the end of this chapter is a list of acceptable tax deductions for business. Consult a tax expert or call the IRS for current allowable deductions. The list is general and will be a good guide so you understand what types of expenses are deductible. It will give you an idea how to keep accurate and complete records to document those expenses.

There are many ways to track expenses. If you deduct any automobile expenses, you must be able to back up the deductions. Whether you have a vehicle used exclusively for business or deduct a percentage of personal car usage, you should keep a log of all expenses—gas, maintenance, etc. If you decide to deduct only the actual mileage, you should keep an accurate log, writing down each business-related trip with mileage and an explanation.

According to several accountants, the IRS attitude concerning deductions such as automobile and home office expenses may change from year to year. While the actual allowable deductions do not change, they may be questioned more and require more documentation in some years than others. A good accountant will help you avoid questionable deductions, while taking full advantage of others.

If you conduct your business from home, you must be very careful about deducting a percentage of your home as a business expense. If the space is used *exclusively* for business you may qualify. This means if you teach in your basement, but it is also used as a family room when you aren't having classes, it cannot be deducted. Do not even consider taking a home office deduction without consulting a reputable tax accountant who deals with home businesses. You can deduct business-related telephone expenses but not a percentage of your base rate, because the IRS assumes you would have a personal phone line anyway. However, a separate line used for business only is deductible.

Setting up Your Books

Once you have contacted an accountant and have a clear picture of what is important, setting up a record keeping system is easy. For a small business with sole proprietorship (one person owner), a checkbook, a ledger for income and expenses and a petty cash fund provide an adequate base for record keeping. You can begin with a simple ledger and an accordionlike folding file, available at most office supply stores. If you have a computer, several excellent bookkeeping and tax accounting programs are available. Check at a computer software store or ask your accountant for a recommendation. No matter what form of record keeping you choose, remember to ask for and keep all receipts. Canceled checks and computer records must be backed up with proof.

Insurance

If you run a business from your home, your insurance agent needs to know about it. A special rider can be added to your homeowner's or renter's policy to cover business-related items in the event of a loss. The addition is not expensive and will cover inventory, business machines and equipment, supplies and more. One painter I know suffered major water damage when pipes running through her attic froze and burst. She lost virtually everything in her painting studio. Books, paints, brushes and surfaces represent a large investment, and if they are used to generate income, they are not covered by a personal policy. Be sure your agent knows exactly what equipment you have. Business machines, such as computers, may need to be covered separately.

Some art and craft associations offer insurance programs to their members covering losses at home or away, including craft shows and malls. Check your library for a directory of organizations and write for information.

Liability Insurance

If you conduct a business where customers come to your home, such as students attending a class, inquire about personal liability coverage. Ask your agent about an umbrella policy to extend your personal liability coverage to include business-related activities.

Banking

It is important to set up a business checking account. With one account for both business and personal affairs, you may be tempted to "rob Peter to pay Paul." Having a checking account for business use only separates business expenses from personal finances and gives a much clearer overall picture of how your business is doing. It also establishes a better credit record for your business, and it simplifies your tax preparation.

Call some local banks and ask what types of accounts are available. Ask about the cost of checks and charges for deposits, bounced checks and anything else that could affect your business. I changed banks because the bank I had used for years began to charge for checks from Canada, even if they were written in U.S. funds. (If you do business in Canada, always request payment in U.S. funds.) When the charge rose to $7.50 per check, I was receiving a good number of individual orders from across the border, so I changed to a bank with no charge for foreign checks. There is also no fee if I receive a "bad" check. Some banks charge up to $20 for a returned check. Surprise charges like that will negatively impact your profits.

Discuss your business needs with a bank officer, and ask what type of account they recommend. You should begin with the least expensive account possible. Some banks offer "linked" accounts. They have no fee as long as a *total* minimum balance is maintained among several accounts. This is ideal if your personal accounts are at the same bank. Even if you deduct bank fees on your business account, it is still money out-of-pocket. It's best to eliminate as many expenses as possible.

Charges for a true business account, which requires a federal ID number from the Department of the Treasury/Internal Revenue Service, may be higher than for a personal checking account. Fees and restrictions vary from bank to bank and are usually different from personal accounts. There seem to be as many variations in bank charges as there are banks, so ask a lot of questions. Large service fees and high charges for printed checks are unnecessary expenses for the start of a small business. If your bank charges are higher for a business account, consider opening a second personal account. Using it for all of your business income and expenses will separate your business and personal expenses for the IRS. It will also show clearly if you are making any profit. Some banks allow you to have your business name on the first line of your checks with your name under it and still not classify it as a business account.

One other option is a DBA (doing business as) account. It is like a personal account and can be opened under your social security number. Under your name there will be a second line that reads DBA, followed by the name of your business. There is usually a set monthly service charge which allows you to make a limited number of transactions with no added fees. This is a good choice for a beginning business because the account has your business name on it, which looks more professional when dealing with suppliers. If your business grows so much the number of transactions you make consistently exceeds the limit, you can visit your banker to discuss changing the account to one more suitable to your needs.

Sales Taxes

In most states, if you buy goods for resale and sell directly to the public at the retail level, you must register your business in your state. You are required to collect and pay sales tax. Contact the sales tax division of the department of revenue for your state. (This has nothing to do with the IRS; it is a state, not federal, tax.) Ask for information on applying for a resale tax number. Some states charge a nominal registration fee, some don't. It may take time for all the paperwork to go through, so don't be alarmed if several months pass before you receive your tax certificate. Once you are registered, you are required to file periodically and pay taxes on goods sold during that period.

Having a tax number has its advantages. It allows you to buy raw materials without paying sales tax at the time of purchase and to buy wholesale from manufacturers and distributors, saving money on supplies. If you sell wholesale, you should have the tax number of each customer in your files.

You may think that if you have a hobby and only sell a few painted pieces at small shows, you do not need to collect and pay sales tax. However, anytime you sell to consumers at a retail level, you must collect sales tax and turn it in to the state. It is illegal to collect sales tax and keep it as part of your profits. If you sell through consignment shops or craft malls, it is their responsibility to collect and pay sales taxes on goods sold.

If you attend shows and sell outside your state, you must pay taxes in the state where the goods are sold. Sales tax rates may vary even within a state because city and county taxes are included. Show management will usually supply tax information to all exhibitors. Some states send representatives around at the end of the show to collect taxes from exhibitors for merchandise sold. In that case, you need to have an accurate sales total by the close of the show.

Even if you pay sales tax when you buy, you must collect it when you sell and turn it in. In most states, sales tax is required when selling to a consumer at the retail level. Some artists prefer to include sales tax in the price of the item, while others add it on at the time of the sale. Either way, be sure to add it in and collect it. If you don't, you still will have to pay at the end of the show, and 7 or 8 percent cuts deeply into your profits.

Buying Supplies Wholesale

Another aspect of good business is buying raw materials at the lowest possible cost. For many years, wholesalers and distributors refused to sell to anyone who did not maintain a storefront business. Over the years this policy has changed considerably. The industry now recognizes that in-home studios and other home-based businesses are an important part of the industry. They are now more open to doing business with decorative painters and other craftspeople.

In some cases there are still large minimums to be met, and this can be a trap for a novice. Although wholesale buying can save a great deal on raw materials, it can also cause you to buy more than you actually need in order to get the lowest price or meet a minimum. It is far better to buy less at a slightly higher price and use all of it than to buy a lot at a lesser price and not use it.

Taking Care of Inventory

One final note on managing supplies and inventory. Take good care of your supply inventory. Wood pieces, painting surfaces and other supplies can represent a large financial investment. Store them properly in an area where they will not be subjected to drastic temperature changes, such as freezing and extreme heat. Try to paint on wood pieces in a timely manner. After storing pieces under the bed for ten or fifteen years, you may be tempted to sell them in a tag sale for far less than their cost. This is lost profit.

Licenses and Permits

When you begin to teach classes or sell your artwork from your home, you become a home-based business. In some communities this means you may be required to have a special license or permit. Usually, if you don't have employees, display a large sign or create a traffic or parking problem with your business, no permit or license is needed. Another factor to keep in mind is that many cities and counties impose an income tax on businesses within their jurisdictions. It would be wise to check with your county clerk or city office to learn what is required in your area.

Keeping It Fun

All of this bookkeeping, banking and tax information may seem to be a lot of hassle for a small business venture. Actually, these few simple steps in the beginning will prevent major headaches later and leave more time for the fun part of your business. Decorative painting is what got you into this, and a good, efficient business plan will allow you more free time to paint and create. If your business blossoms and grows, you will be well prepared to take the growth in stride.

With your business now in good order, it's time to find out how to increase it so it fulfills your dreams and expectations.

*T*hese should be verified with an accountant to be sure they have not changed and are acceptable for your business.

ALLOWABLE DEDUCTIONS FOR BUSINESS EXPENSES

Accounting or bookkeeping

Advertising

Automobile (if used for business)

Bad debts (uncollected accounts, bad checks)

Business gifts

Commissions (sales reps, other sellers)

Consulting fees

Conventions and trade shows

Donations

Dues (business-related organizations)

Education (classes, seminars, books, business-related magazines and periodicals)

Entertainment (business related)

Equipment (lease or purchase, expense or depreciation)

Freight and shipping charges

Insurance premiums

Interest on business loans, bank charges, etc.

IRA or Keogh deposits

Labor costs

Legal fees

Licenses or permits

Office furnishings

Office supplies

Postage

Refunds

Rent and utilities specifically related to business

Research and development

Supplies and materials

Taxes

Tax preparer's fee

Travel (business related)

Wages to employees

CHAPTER EIGHT

Getting the Word Out—Good Advertising

MANY TECHNIQUES FOR PROMOTING your decorative painting skills have been covered in previous chapters because they were specific to a particular application of your capabilities. There are a few important things, however, that apply to virtually every form of business.

Maintaining an Image

Let's begin with the image you project. It is crucial to create and maintain an image that clearly says you are a professional, not just a hobbyist. This will make a better impression on clients, and it will help family and friends understand that you require enough time to maintain your business. Friends and relatives can unintentionally undermine your business by making demands on your time. Repeated interruptions can drastically cut down on your productivity. If you set aside certain hours of the day for your business, stick to them. Discourage social phone calls and drop-in company during that time. Unfortunately, leisure time is often one of the casualties of a home-based business, but efficient use of working hours will help free up time for fun. If you sell to companies who maintain regular business hours, you must be available for business during those hours.

Business Materials

Having well-designed, classy looking printed materials is one way to project a businesslike image. An unusual, memorable business card, a well-designed letterhead with matching envelopes on high-quality stock and an attractive brochure all indicate that you are a professional. Even if you are on a limited budget, you should invest in business cards, and do it with style. Your business card is an important promotional tool and speaks volumes about who you are. If necessary, hire a professional to help you create a card with the image you want to project. When your business grows, you can have the same design repeated on stationery and other business forms.

Your card should include the name of your business, your name, address and/or telephone number and possibly a line that describes what you do. On any business materials, including checks, if you list an address, be sure to include the zip code, and list the area code with your telephone number. Other information you might add are a fax number, an E-mail address and a Web site address.

Free Local Advertising Opportunities

Use every opportunity to promote your business. Many city newspapers use feature stories on interesting businesses run by local people. Local television stations or cable networks may do the same, or they may have openings for guest demonstrators on a home decorating show.

Donating artwork to charitable causes, such as fund-raising auctions, can pay big dividends by introducing your name and work to attendees. Remember my earlier advice to donate your best work, not your worst. This is a form of advertising, and donating the "dogs" that no one else wanted conveys a poor image.

Participate in any art show that includes decorative painting. Even if you don't win "Best of the Show," you may win new customers. Enter your work at the fair. Some tole chapters of the Society of Decorative Painters sponsor a booth at the fair featuring examples of decorative painting as a way to promote membership in the Society. Offer to do a demonstration in your area of expertise. Libraries often have space for month-long exhibits featuring local artists. If none of these opportunities exist in your area, try to be instrumental in getting them started.

Another excellent way to expose your talents locally is to offer to decorate an area in a local hospital or school. Decorative painters are known for their willingness to share their talents to benefit charitable organizations. It is almost always a win-win situation.

Paid Advertising

Occasionally word-of-mouth and free advertising are simply not enough. If you find you are not reaching a broad enough market or the response to the free advertising is too weak, you may have to bite the bullet and invest in paid advertising offering better results. Be sure the method of advertising you choose reaches the people interested in what you offer. No matter how reasonable the rates, if your message doesn't reach the right market, it is a waste of money. I know one quaint gift shop owner who bought radio time based strictly on finding the station offering the most air time for the least money. Unfortunately, advertising a country gift and antique shop on a hard rock station aimed at teenagers produced no response whatsoever. Study the marketplace before you invest. Advertise classes within the general area where you plan to teach. Advertise books and packets in publications geared to people who paint. Use common sense.

It's also a good idea to check with other advertisers to learn how good their results have been. Weigh the income potential against the amount of the investment. Also remember that one-shot advertising does not pay off as well as repetition.

Mailing Lists

Compile a mailing list, and keep customers and students advised of any upcoming events. If you use a mailing list, keep it current. Delete the names of people who never show an interest, and add new ones whenever possible. If you own a computer, consider investing in mail list software. It is inexpensive and makes compiling and organizing customer mailing lists a snap. It will also print address labels, which is much faster than addressing materials by hand. If you add a sales code (e.g., include Dept. 999 in the return address), you can tell in just minutes how many people are responding to your mail-out and how profitable it is. If you do not have a computer, use individual file cards to record your customer list, with notations on each card to track a customer's buying habits and special interests.

When you participate in craft shows, the show sponsors should handle advertising, but it never hurts to drop postcards in the mail to tell your customers where you will be. Passing out or posting flyers in local businesses is another good way to alert people about your future plans, such as classes, workshops or sales.

Using the Internet

There is no doubt the Internet will become an even larger marketing tool than it already is. New technology indicates it will eventually be hooked to our TV sets, allowing even broader access. It will become as much a way of life for most people as watching television. Even if you haven't thought about going on-line, give it some thought for the future. Many decorative artists already promote their packets and books via the Internet, and they are excited about the results.

Conclusion

IN WRITING THIS BOOK, I remembered and discovered several things. The first is, I truly love the world decorative painting has opened for me. It has given me wonderful opportunities. The excitement of achieving a variety of goals and introducing me to many wonderful people I would otherwise have missed knowing in my lifetime are added bonuses. For me, the joys of teaching have been far more than I can adequately convey, but I have thoroughly enjoyed all aspects of this business. The possible exception to my enjoyment would be deadlines, but without deadlines, I might not have achieved anything at all.

Many years ago, I was working on my first effort at self-publishing a book. There was a man seated next to me on a plane who, after looking over my shoulder at my tiny layout drawings, asked what I was doing. When I told him I was working on a book, he said he frequently sat down at his computer and wrote things he thought might later be used in a book. He told me one of the rewards of writing is that you often discover you know far more than you realized. My rather smug reply was that, being a teacher, that probably wouldn't happen to me. I had to keep all of my knowledge right up front so I could share it with students.

Well, need I tell you how surprised I was to learn every time I have put together a book of any kind, I have had the experience the man spoke of? We *all* know far more than we realize. Tap into that knowledge! It will surprise you and carry you farther than you imagine possible.

If you don't already know it, decorative painting is based on sharing your knowledge through a positive form of teaching. This sharing attitude spills over into other aspects of the business. Most decorative painters I have met are not just willing but eager to help. They know the art will only grow and evolve through creative energy. Sharing through teaching and publishing stoke the fires of creativity.

Don't be afraid to try anything you think you can handle, but keep your goals realistic. Success is usually achieved in increments, not all at once. Begin with a good business plan and stick to it. Positioning your goals slightly beyond your reach will keep you striving to improve. If you don't always reach your goal on the first try, regroup and try again. The anticipation of success is sometimes more exciting than actually achieving success. Sit back and enjoy the ride!

Society of Decorative Painters

393 N. McLean Blvd., Wichita, KS 67203-5968, (316) 269-9300

Helan Barrick

5805 E. 78th Pl., Tulsa, OK 74136, (918) 492-2218

Nora Blair

7364 Etowah Drive, Riverdale, GA 30296, (770) 997-4565

Gail Bremer

4159 S. 76th St., Milwaukee, WI 53220, (414) 321-6611

Barbara Buttram

100 W. Twin Oaks, Broken Arrow, OK 74011, (918) 451-1972

Gretchen Cagle, Gretchen Cagle Publications, Inc.

P.O. Box 2104, Claremore, OK 74018-2104, (918) 342-1080

Carolyn Curry

8508 E. 24 Place, Tulsa, OK 74129, (918) 627-9194

Lynne Deptula & Judy Diephouse, Distinctive Brushstrokes

1674 Hall SE, Grand Rapids, MI 49506

Sylvia Eaton

1818 Salem Rd., Mt. Vernon, IL 62864, (618) 244-0125

Andy Jones & Phillip C. Myer, PCM Studios

731 Highland Ave. NE, Suite D, Atlanta, GA 30312-1425, (404) 222-0348

Karen LaStracco

106 S. Pecan, Nacogdoches, TX 75961, (409) 569-1929

Diana Marcum

RR1, Box 1445, Otterville, MD 65348-8846, (816) 366-4245

Carol Mays
6502 W. 51st St., Tulsa, OK 74107, (918) 446-8625

Peggy Nuttall
441 Claremont Dr., Norman, OK 73069, (405) 329-6646

Pat Olson
624 Kentucky, Sturgeon Bay, WI 54235, (920) 743-8148

Cynde J. Paveglio
1818 3rd St., Bay City, MI 48708, (517) 892-8730

Gloria Perkins
236 Craig Wood Way, Sharpsburg, GA 30277, (770) 463-3300

Linda Pinion
5317 E. 7th, Tulsa, OK 74112, 918-835-5149

Jay Sharp, Creative Painting Convention
P.O. Box 80720, Las Vegas, NV 89180, (702) 221-8234

Index

More Great Books for Decorative Painters!

Acrylic Decorative Painting Techniques—Discover stroke-by-stroke instruction that takes you through the basics and beyond! More than 50 fun and easy painting techniques are illustrated in simple demonstrations that offer at least two variations on each method. Plus, a thorough discussion on tools, materials, color, preparation and backgrounds. #30884/$24.99/128 pages/550 color illus.

Painting & Decorating Birdhouses—Turn unfinished birdhouses into something special—from a quaint Victorian roost to a Southwest pueblo, from a rustic log cabin to a lighthouse! These colorful and easy decorative painting projects are for the birds with 22 clever projects to create indoor decorative birdhouses, as well as functional ones to grace your garden. #30882/$23.99/128 pages/194 color illus./paperback

Decorative Painting Sourcebook—Priscilla Hauser, Phillip Myer and Jackie Shaw lend their expertise to this one-of-a-kind guide straight from the pages of *Decorative Artist's Workbook*! You'll find step-by-step, illustrated instructions on every technique—from basic brushstrokes to faux finishes, painting glassware, wood, clothing and much more! #30883/$24.99/128 pages/200 color illus./paperback

The Decorative Stamping Sourcebook—Embellish walls, furniture, fabric and accessories—with stamped designs! You'll find 180 original, traceable motifs in a range of themes and illustrated instructions for making your own stamps to enhance any decorating style. #30898/$24.99/128 pages/200 color illus.

Master Strokes—Master the techniques of decorative painting with this comprehensive guide! Learn to use decorative paint finishes on everything from small objects and furniture to walls and floors, including dozens of step-by-step demonstrations and numerous techniques. #30937/$22.99/160 pages/400 color illus./paperback

The Best of Silk Painting—Discover inspiration in sophisticated silk with this gallery of free-flowing creativity. Over 100 full-color photos capture the glorious colors, unusual textures and unique designs of 77 talented artists. #30840/$29.99/128 pages/136 color illus.

Painting Houses, Cottages and Towns on Rocks—Discover how a dash of paint can turn humble stones into charming cottages, churches, Victorian mansions and more. This hands-on, easy-to-follow book offers a menagerie of fun—and potentially profitable—stone animal projects. Eleven examples, complete with material list, photos of the finished piece and patterns will help you create entire rock villages. #30823/$21.99/128 pages/398 color illus./paperback

Decorative Painting With Gretchen Cagle—Discover decorative painting at its finest as you browse through pages of charming motifs. You'll brighten walls, give life to old furniture, create unique accent pieces and special gifts using step-by-step instructions, traceable drawings, detailed color mixes and more! #30803/$24.99/144 pages/64 color, 36 b&w illus./paperback

Creative Paint Finishes for Furniture—Revive your furniture with fresh color and design! Inexpensive, easy and fun painting techniques are at your fingertips, along with step-by-step directions and a photo gallery of imaginative applications for faux finishing, staining, stenciling, mosaic, découpage and many other techniques. #30748/$27.99/144 pages/236 color, 7 b&w illus.

Creative Paint Finishes for the Home—A complete, full-color step-by-step guide to decorating floors, walls and furniture—including how to use the tools, master the techniques and develop ideas. #30426/$27.99/144 pages/212 color illus.

Master Works: How to Use Paint Finishes to Transform Your Surroundings—Discover how to use creative paint finishes to enhance and excite the "total look" of your home. This step-by-step guide contains dozens of exciting ideas on fresco, marbling, paneling and other simple paint techniques for bringing new life to any space. Plus, you'll also find innovative uses for fabrics, screens and blinds. #30626/$29.95/176 pages/150 color illus.

Create Your Own Greeting Cards and Gift Wrap with Priscilla Hauser—You'll see sponge prints, eraser prints, cellophane scrunching, marbleizing, paper making and dozens of other techniques you can use to make unique greetings for all your loved ones. #30621/$24.99/128 pages/230 color illus.

Stencil Source Book 2—Add color and excitement to fabrics, furniture, walls and more with over 200 original motifs that can be used again and again! Idea-packed chapters will help you create dramatic color schemes and themes to enhance your home in hundreds of ways. #30730/$22.99/144 pages/300 illus.

The Crafts Supply Sourcebook, 4th edition—Turn here to find the materials you need—from specialty tools and the hardest-to-find accessories, to clays, doll parts, patterns, quilting machines and hundreds of other items! Listings organized by area of interest make it quick and easy! #70344/$18.99/320 pages/paperback

Paint Craft—Discover great ideas for enhancing your home, wardrobe and personal items. You'll see how to master the basics of mixing and planning colors, how to print with screen and linoleum to create your own stationery, how to enhance old glassware and pottery pieces with unique patterns and motifs and much more! #30678/$16.95/144 pages/200 color illus./paperback

Nature Craft—Dozens of step-by-step nature craft projects to create, including dried flower garlands, baskets, corn dollies, potpourri and more. Bring the outdoors inside with these wonderful projects crafted with readily available natural materials. #30531/$16.99/144 pages/200 color illus./paperback

Paper Craft—Dozens of step-by-step paper craft projects to make, including greeting cards, boxes and desk sets, jewelry and pleated paper blinds. If you have ever worked with or wanted to work with paper you'll enjoy these attractive, fun-to-make projects. #30530/$16.95/144 pages/200 color illus./paperback

Everything You Ever Wanted to Know About Fabric Painting—Discover how to create beautiful fabrics! You'll learn how to set up work space, choose materials, plus the ins and outs of tie-dye, screen printing, woodgraining, marbling, cyanotype and more! #30625/$21.99/128 pages/4-color throughout/paperback

Painting Murals—Learn through eight step-by-step projects how to choose a subject for a mural, select colors that will create the desired effects and transfer the design to the final surface. #30081/$29.99/168 pages/125 color illus.